Soul Food

Also by Eric V. Copage

Kwanzaa: An African-American Celebration
of Culture and Cooking

Black Pearls

Black Pearls for Parents

Black Pearls Journal

Black Pearls Book of Love

A Kwanzaa Fable

Soul Food

INSPIRATIONAL

STORIES FOR

AFRICAN AMERICANS

Eric V. Copage

HYPERION NEW YORK

A list of permissions, constituting a continuation of the copyright page,
appears on pages 263–269.

Copyright © 2000 Eric V. Copage

Library of Congress Cataloging-in-Publication Data
Copage, Eric V.
Soul food: inspirational stories for African American / Eric V. Copage—1st ed.
p.   cm.
ISBN: 0-7868-8499-1 (trade pbk.)
1. Afro-Americans—Conduct of life—Anecdotes.
2. Spiritual life—Anecdotes. 3. Social values—United States—Anecdotes.
4. Inspiration—Anecdotes. 5. Afro-Americans—Biography—Anecdotes.
I. Title.

E185.86.C58212 2000
158'.089'96073—dc21   00–027226

Designed by Abby Kagan

FIRST EDITION

2   4   6   8   10   9   7   5   3   1

To my father, John E. Copage,

whose stories of his youth and young adulthood

continue to inspire me and give me strength.

And to my children, Evan and Siobhán,

whose ongoing stories renew my life daily.

CONTENTS

CONTENTS

FAMILY

CREATIVITY

CONTENTS

CONTENTS

FAITH

INTRODUCTION

❦

"TELL ME A STORY" was one of the first sentences out of my mouth. (At least that is what I've been told; perhaps it's only a story!) But I do remember well my toddlerhood, and asking for endless repetitions of *How the Grinch Stole Christmas*, Aesop's fables, and an East Indian story, the name of which is lost to me now, but its central image was of the youngest of three brothers getting what he wants by focusing solely on the target. As time went on I read and reread stories to myself— Langston Hughes's Simple stories, Julius Lester's rendition of the Uncle Remus stories, Zen parables, and Hasidic tales where everyday bric-a -brac stood for more than their earthly appearances.

What did these disparate tales have in common? They warmed my heart and nourished my soul. The observations of Jesse Simple validated my observations of the world—and did it with a smile. These stories made it so that I didn't feel alone. And even as an adult, reading about the trickery of Brer Rabbit over his larger and more lethal foes fortified me for my interactions with a world that often seemed unfair and uncaring.

Not all my stories came from books. My father would regale me with tales of his childhood on the wrong side of the tracks in Depression-era Chicago. He would tell me tales of gangs, how he and his brother and his mother managed through deprivation—and a haunted apartment he once lived in!

Whether my father meant to or not—and he told his stories casually, not with a great fanfare—he gave me with his stories a watering hole for my psyche, a spiritual oasis where I could gather strength for my own forays into the world. They were minihugs, psychic embraces. They were a small voice in my ear saying, "Yes you can! There is a way. You can turn this to your advantage!"

One story I especially remember is of how my father, at one time in his life, came to be fluent in Italian. It wasn't that he was planning to be a Berlitz teacher or was ginning up for a tour of the great artworks of Rome. Rather, he learned that particular language because there was a lot of ethnic violence in Chicago at that time. He discovered that speaking a little of their ancestral tongue so disarmed the Italians that they let him go about his business (though my father never told me about how he coped with the Irish or the Poles).

In compiling this book's selection of stories I went looking for tales that would provide spiritual sustenance. Most are no more than one thousand words because I wanted these stories to be a nutritious meal, but not a nine-course banquet that would take days to finish. I have on occasion included a quote, a poem, or a list—snacks, if you will—for readers who don't want a sit-down dinner at that moment but still want something to munch on. But for the most part this book is comprised of short narratives so the reader can become engrossed in the action, but complete the reading in fifteen minutes or so.

Some stories are excerpted from autobiographies of black luminaries, including Patti LaBelle and Colin Powell. There are fables of Aesop and folk tales from the Caribbean, the United States, and Africa. There are also stories from acclaimed, young, and up-and-coming writers such as Veronica Chambers and Jacqueline Jones LaMon, and from people from various walks of life who heard about the book and wanted to contribute stories from their lives they felt would fit under one of the chapter headings: Love, Self-esteem, Family, Creativity, Tenacity, Wisdom, and Faith. Some of these people used their own names; some used pseudonyms; and some asked me to be their scribe.

What attracted me to the material I've included varies depending on the story. One of my favorites is the first excerpt from the joint autobiography of Ossie Davis and Ruby Dee. I was especially attracted to the idea that the smallest concrete gesture could speak louder about love than volumes of the grandest love poetry, or boxes of the sweetest chocolates. In the chapter on self-esteem, I was attracted by the strength and nobility of Queen Latifah, who emphasizes using self-esteem not as a crutch of self-satisfaction, but as a prod to achieve greater and greater things.

It's a truism at this point that one's family is not necessarily comprised of biological relatives, but those with whom you share a psychological and cultural connection as well. That is the point Langston Hughes makes so eloquently in his poem about being a kinsman with those of African descent be they from Africa, Kentucky, or the West Indies. What is less acknowledged, or in some quarters even accepted, is that you needn't agree with everything a family member has to say. You may disagree, but still love that person fiercely. That is the point of the story by Michel Marriott, a *New York Times* reporter, as he describes being pledged for the Omega Psi Phi Fraternity, or the Q's.

Jon Haggins, a New York–based journalist, television host, and tour operator, shows in one of his tales how if you keep pedaling toward your dream, you will eventually reach it. And Sonsyrea Tate, a writer and Washington, D.C.–based elementary schoolteacher, reveals how, with a little faith, even the most dire situations can be overcome. I could go on. The recipes at the end of each chapter give the reader a summary of some of the points gleaned from the preceding stories. Sometimes, something new is tossed in for fun.

And one other thing to note: The titles I use for the stories and excerpts are mostly made up by me to highlight one aspect of the writing. So if you don't think one fits just right, try an alternative title. There is a lot to be learned from each one of these pieces, far more than can be compressed into an image or a phrase.

This book may be read cover to cover like a formal meal. Or you can leaf through the book and snack on what you are in the mood for at the moment. Or you can belly up to it like a buffet table and take helping after helping of your favorite dish. Or you can take the recipes and create your own repast.

So go on, flip through the book. And enjoy soul food you find here and elsewhere. Guaranteed low cholesterol and good for the heart.

ERIC V. COPAGE

Love

THE GREATNESS
OF SMALL GESTURES

T HERE WAS NO BIG CEREMONY, no wedding
gown, no church service, no pictures. There had
not even been a discussion of where we would
live. It felt almost like an appointment we finally got
around to keeping.

After the "I promises," the "I dos," and the tears, my
maid of honor, Ossie's best man, Ossie, and I got on the bus
bound from Jersey City back to New York City. I wore a
brown suit. Ossie wore a hat and carried his overcoat.

For the whole trip, Ossie's body was twisted from the
waist as he gazed out the window. I looked out the window,
too, and then I looked at him, out the window, and at his
porkpie hat—back and forth like that. Neither of us spoke.
He didn't look back at me.

A kind of low-grade panic came over me. So this is it.
We are married. Related now. Connected. Forever and

ever, maybe. I felt a silence all through me. The bus was moving, but there was no sound. "As long as you both shall live . . ." Maybe this is what forever feels like. Maybe I was just hungry. All of us should be hungry. It had been a long day even though it was just after noon.

We ate at a restaurant near my sister's apartment. After the meal, my bridesmaid, LaVerne, asked, "Where will you guys be living?" I didn't recall having discussed it, but Ossie answered without hesitation, "At my place in the Bronx."

"Oh, yes" she said, "I've got that number." And we hugged, and kissed, and went our separate ways.

There had been confusion in my mind. I had wanted him to come live with me at my mother's apartment because his room in the Bronx seemed always in total disarray. When I visited Ossie, he would have to clear spaces for me to sit and put my things on. Newspapers, books, magazines, toilet articles, clothes, orange peelings were everywhere. The space was not dusty or dirty, as I recall, only extremely cluttered.

We went by taxi to Mother's place, where I packed a few things. He understood that there just simply hadn't been time to properly move, with rehearsals every day, and so much going on in both our lives. We had talked about getting an apartment but we'd soon be traveling with *The Smile of the World* and that could last a long time.

I said to myself, How could you think, Ruby, that he's even thought about moving in with you and your mother? What a thick-headed contemplation.

As we walked up the one flight to our love nest, I felt ashamed of my reluctance.

"We jumped the broom," he said. "May as well carry you over the threshold." And he did—into one of the cleanest, neatest spaces I could hope for. Not only that, but Pat, his landlady, had turned another room into a lounge area for us where she had prepared and left food and drinks. "Well, you know I couldn't bring my bride into the place like it was before, now could I?"

I hugged him then and started to cry. He pushed me an arm's length away and looked at me a long time; and when our eyes met, we laughed, and laughed, and laughed.

RUBY DEE,
from *With Ossie and Ruby*

TO THINE OWN SELF
BE TRUE

⚜

S OMETIMES WE CAN LET the ghosts of the past, even when it is not our own past, haunt us. That was the case with Patti LaBelle. Her father had been a rambler and a ladies' man, and it was this ghost that almost kept the young Patti LaBelle from the fulfilling thirty-year marriage she enjoys with her husband, Armstead. She had refused to make a commitment to him, and finally, after several times, he said he would not ask her again. That is when reality hit—a life without her soul mate. And so she took the bull by the horns and asked him to marry her. But she didn't get to that point easily or without pain. She had to look deep into her soul. In her own words:

What I do know is that when I told Armstead I had broken my engagement [with Otis William of the Temptations] he seemed unusually happy. I was still feeling guilty about the breakup and sometimes, not often but sometimes, I wondered if I had made the right decision. It wasn't just that I had broken up with a great guy who treated me well. Let's be real here: Otis was one of the most eligible bachelors in the country, rich, famous, and internationally adored. Part of me thought I was crazy. Armstead's support helped me get through it. He said the same thing Chubby (Mother) did—that I had to follow my heart—but he took it one step further.

"You can't live your life for other people," he told me. "You have to be true to yourself."

PATTI LABELLE,
from *Don't Block the Blessings*

CUPID'S ARROW

❧

I MET MY HUSBAND in the off season on Oak Bluffs, a cozy neighborhood on Martha's Vineyard, an island just off the coast of Massachusetts, where blacks have been summering for generations. It's quiet in the fall, and we had independently gone up there to meditate, to think about new directions for our lives, and to enjoy the crisp salt sea air of autumn.

When we first laid eyes on each other, we knew we were destined to get married. His grandparents owned a house on the island, and he had visited there every summer his whole life. He showed me around. He picked up from the ground a twig the length of his forearm and told me how he and his younger brother would fix twigs with string or a rubber band and pretend to be Indians hunting with bows and arrows. He playfully held the twig like a bow and let loose an imaginary arrow at my heart. He accompanied me back to the inn where I was staying, carrying the stick with him. A teddy bear with a violet ribbon around its neck sat on the fireplace mantel in the living room. He removed the ribbon, tied it into a bow near the top of the stick, and using a plain ballpoint pen wrote the words *Oak Bluffs, Martha's Vineyard*, then handed it to me saying simply, "A souvenir." I couldn't have been happier had he given me a jeweled scepter.

We were married on the island a year later, and our marriage has been filled with much happiness, loving friends, three children. And although the stick disappeared during one of our many moves as we relocated during my husband's frequent promotions, we always returned to the island, spending August there.

On our twenty-fifth wedding anniversary we had a real southern celebration—lots of food, music, laughing, and dancing. Among the many gifts was a baton-shaped object. Judging from the crinkled wrapping paper, the gift giver hadn't bothered to put the object into a box. Though that present caught my eye first, I opened it last. The first thing I saw when I peeled back the paper was a lavender bow, and as I continued peeling, I saw the letters O-A-K. It turns out that because of our frequent moves, my husband had put the stick in our safe deposit box so that it wouldn't get lost. He glanced at the stick and then looked at me with tears in his eyes. I opened my mouth to speak, and cried.

AS TOLD TO ERIC V. COPAGE

THE COMMITMENT

BY TRADITION, the first wedding anniversary is paper, the second cotton, the third leather, and so forth. But my wife and I from the very start of our marriage ten years ago set out to make every anniversary a diamond jubilee. The first anniversary we celebrated simply with a dinner at the restaurant where we had first met for a drink. But since we were better off, this time we splurged on their best champagne. On the second anniversary, to show that we were more in love with each other than before, we went to a four-star restaurant, had a much more expensive dinner, and treated ourselves to a bottle of *their* best champagne. By the third anniversary, dinner was not enough. The evening of our anniversary began with a fifty-dollar horsedrawn carriage ride through the park, then an expensive dinner, and ended with a gondola ride in a park lake by moonlight. Our fourth anniversary took us away from our city, and occupied a whole weekend.

We headed for the Poconos—bubble baths, heart-shaped tubs, rose-covered satin sheets. The works. And so, we increased the ante of our wedding anniversary each year. Last year was no exception. We were set to spend a week in the Bahamas. We had saved for nearly six months for the treat, and had paid all the deposits on it.

Then my brother rang. Well, not literally my brother, but a cousin so dear and close and good that he feels like the best brother anybody can have. He told me he needed extra hands for the soup kitchen where he volunteers. They were having a special celebration for the founder of the church that runs the kitchen. My brother has never asked me for anything—only given—so I jumped at the chance to return many an unreturned favor. And the timing would be no problem—the celebration was several days before our departure for the Bahamas. I'd be there, ladle at the ready, I said. I told my wife, and she agreed she'd be on hand also. I felt that I had finally in some small measure repaid him for his past kindnesses.

He called the next day. He asked if I could be there earlier in the evening than previously arranged. I said no problem. He signed off with, "I'll see you on the ninth." The ninth? I thought. Hadn't he said the fifth during our last call? On the ninth my wife and I would be in the Bahamas celebrating our wedding anniversary. My brother must have heard or felt a hesitation from my end of the line. He asked, "If something has come up on your end, I can still make other arrangements." I quickly said

I'd be there at the new time and hung up. I didn't know what to do. I didn't want to disappoint my brother, nor did I want to disappoint my wife and torpedo our tradition.

But truth be told, that tradition had become frayed of late. Our friends thought that our anniversaries were oh so romantic, and at first they were. But with each year I was beginning to find its increasing ostentation burdensome—the planning, the expense. It was almost becoming like Christmas—a frenetic display rather than a meditation on the meaning of something sacred.

How to break this to my wife, since we had planned and saved, and looked forward to the trip. And most especially, we had paid for most of it already. But when I told her I thought we should honor our commitment to my brother, she heartily agreed. Turns out she was feeling the burden of ostentation also, and felt our anniversaries were beginning to deteriorate into a flurry of empty gestures. During that conversation, we reconnected. We rediscovered each other.

We showed up on the ninth, aprons on, ladles in hand. We doled out a hot meal of chicken, string beans, yams, and pecan pie to hundreds of people. We listened with tears in our eyes to testimony from mothers, old people, and people just down on their luck on how the soup kitchen had been a vital part of their life. A lifesaver in the most literal sense. We drove home and on the way, my wife and I discussed our anniversary. This one was truly special. We vowed not to try to repeat it, nor top it, but in the future to take it easy, and to look for gentle ways to reconsecrate our love for each other. We reached our house. It was dark. The children were staying at their grandparents. My wife and I entered, lit a couple of candles, and uncorked a decent bottle of red wine. We put Marvin Gaye on the CD. We fed each other chocolates and strawberries. Then we made love and made love and made love and made love and made love the way we hadn't in years.

AS TOLD TO ERIC V. COPAGE

RESIGNATION

I love you
because the Earth turns round the sun
because the North wind blows north
sometimes
because the Pope is Catholic
and most Rabbis Jewish
because winters flow into springs
and the air clears after a storm
because only my love for you
despite the charms of gravity
keeps me from falling off this Earth
into another dimension
I love you
because it is the natural order of things

*   *   *

I love you
like the habit I picked up in college
of sleeping through lectures
or saying I'm sorry
when I get stopped for speeding
because I drink a glass of water
in the morning
and chain-smoke cigarettes
all through the day
because I take my coffee Black
and my milk with chocolate
because you keep my feet warm
though my life a mess
I love you because I don't want it
any other way

I am helpless
in my love for you
It makes me so happy
to hear you call my name
I am amazed you can resist
locking me in an echo chamber
where your voice reverberates
through the four walls
sending me into spasmatic ecstasy
I love you
because it's been so good
for so long
that if I didn't love you

I'd have to be born again
and that is not a theological statement
I am pitiful in my love for you

The Dells tell me love
is so simple
the thought though of you
sends indescribably delicious multitudinous
thrills throughout and through-in my body
I love you
because no two snowflakes are alike
and it is possible
if you stand tippy-toe
to walk between the raindrops
I love you
because I am afraid of the dark
and can't sleep in the light
because I rub my eyes
when I wake up in the morning
and find you there
because you with all your magic powers were
determined that
I should love you
because there was nothing for you but that
I would love you
I love you
because you made me
want to love you
more than I love my privacy

my freedom my commitments
and responsibilities
I love you 'cause I changed my life
to love you
because you saw me one Friday
afternoon and decided that I would
love you
I love you I love you I love you

N I K K I   G I O V A N N I ,
from *Love Poems*

NOT SUCH A BITTER PILL

⁂

THE VOICE set my teeth on edge, like hearing a rake scraping against concrete or fingernails drawn across a chalkboard. The voice was that of my wife's elderly aunt. Since the moment of my wife's birth, that same voice had been a solace to my wife in times of trouble. After her parents divorced. After her father and brother, my wife's only other sibling, had died in a car crash. After her mother's painful death from cancer. It had shared the intimacy of my wife's first menstrual cycle, first boyfriend, first kiss. It had been a balm to the terrors of a complicated pregnancy. While I heard a pounding jackhammer as her lips formed to make the vowels and consonants that came tumbling from her mouth, my wife heard melodies from a celeste.

I cannot completely explain why the woman got on my nerves. Part of it might have been her relentless cheerfulness. She had an old corny saying for every situation. Jealousy, too, might have been a factor. She had known my wife far longer than I had. She had shared verbal intimacies that would be difficult for any man to compete with.

I did my best to avoid the woman. When she called, I handed the phone to my wife with nary a hello. When she rang at the door to pick up my wife for a shopping mission, as they called it, I was brusque almost to the point of rudeness. And when she came over for drinks or dinner, I would suddenly find something that urgently needed doing—like taking out the trash—and slip out of the house.

My behavior hurt my wife. I knew this. But despite loving her, I couldn't change. Or felt I couldn't change. Part of it was inertia, part of it was stubborness, and part of it was that I just didn't like the woman.

My wife didn't complain, though. I think she knew it was useless, but I could see by the disappointed look in her eyes, a look that seemed to say, "Why can't my best friends be friends?" But as much as I loved my wife, I couldn't face having a conversation with that woman.

Then one day, my wife had to go to the hospital to have an operation. It should have been routine, but something went wrong. Over the hours, then days, my wife's life was in danger. Then through her slow recovery, her aunt showed up faithfully. And I remained faithfully silent, except for grunting a hello.

On the seventh day, I was returning to the ward from getting a sandwich. I was in the elevator when I heard steps racing toward the closing doors. I pressed DOOR OPEN

and saw her. My wife's aunt. I had half a mind to punch
DOOR CLOSED. But it was too late. I was stuck with her for a
snail-like ride to my wife's room. We were going seven
floors up, but I felt as if I were descending nine. And when
my wife's aunt opened her mouth to thank me, my head
began to throb with the cacophony of a thousand con-
struction sites.

After her thanks, she asked me a question. Thinking of
my wife, her state, my love for my wife, and that the aunt
and I would be in her presence together in just a moment
or two, I answered as politely as I could. Apparently surprised and encouraged by this, the aunt asked another
question, and another. And I answered. I noticed that
being polite to this woman—Beverly was her name—
wasn't so bad after all. I mustered a question. The elevator
doors opened, but I continued listening to her answer. And
to my surprise, I asked Beverly another question. And
another. As we were walking toward my wife's room we
were actually having a conversation. My wife, still under
medication, looked at us, surprised at first. And then she
beamed. It must have seemed like a dream to her in more
ways than one. Actually witnessing my wife's reaction
brought home to me how important it was for her two best
friends to get along.

It was not happily ever after with Beverly. It's not that I
looked forward to hearing her on the phone, or opening
the door and seeing her standing there, or having dinner
together. Or listening to her corny sayings. But I no longer
rankled at the thought of Beverly. In fact, there was a
sneaking affection. I found out she wasn't such a bad old

gal after all. But what made me want to find some place in my heart for Aunt Beverly was the enormous place in my heart I had for my wife. And our love. I still remember the look on her face when she saw Aunt Beverly and me heading toward her in conversation. It was a look of joy that still makes my soul sing.

AS TOLD TO ERIC V. COPAGE

YOU'RE NOBODY 'TIL YOU'VE GOT SOMEBODY TO LOVE

W HEN YOU'RE A SINGLE GUY and you finish that show, no matter how loudly people applaud for you or how many of them you have up to your place afterward, sooner or later everybody else goes home. You've got nobody to give you security, nobody to root for, nobody rooting for you. You've got no reason for doing the hundred and one things you do automatically when you're in love.

SAMMY DAVIS JR.

MORE PRECIOUS THAN GOLD

THINK OF THE GOLD RING, beloved. Whether it adorns the finger of an auto mechanic or the chairman of General Motors, its ultimate origins come from the earth.

Think of the gold bar, beloved. Whether it is possessed by a banker or a thief it has undergone the same process of heating and molding.

Think of the gold coin, beloved. Whether it is in the palm of a movie celebrity or that of an office secretary, the designer who designed it, the machine that stamped it did so with no care of whose hand would find it.

Know that you are gold, beloved, your inner essence always shining. And remember, beloved, that no matter what your circumstances, you will always be treasured in the eyes of God.

PATRICIA ROBINSON

THE PRIZE

More than a quarter of a century after the fact, I can still feel the tears. They are welling up inside me right now as I'm sorting through the Barbie dolls and Easy Bake ovens of a childhood cocooned in dust. I am in my mother's attic, weeping. But this afternoon's tears are tears of love, not the tears of bitterness that ran down my cheeks when I was a sophomore in high school.

My family moved to a rich white suburb of Los Angeles in the late sixties, just as I was about to enter high school. We had lived in an all-black middle-class community, but with the social tumult and calls for housing integration, my mother decided that I and my younger sister—the two weird sisters, she would joke—should take advantage of this strange new world that suddenly became available. A world where the students not only had a parking lot, but a

covered parking garage (remember, this was sunny southern California!), as well as an Olympic-size pool and a
planetarium funded not by property taxes or sales tax
from the lacquered shops frequented by their lacquered
clientele, but by a looming presence overlooking the athletic field—an oil field and working rig, which nodded,
like a giant grasshopper ceaselessly pumping money into
the band uniforms, and salaries of teachers with doctor-
ates. So we moved to a small Spanish stucco house just
within the Beverly Hills city limits.

I knew the sacrifices my mother had made to get us
there, and I knew I was supposed to set an example for my
nine-year-old sister. I worked hard to excel and I did excel.
I got straight As. I also loved sports. My mother didn't like
the idea of me participating in sports. "White people
think that sports is the only thing we can do," she ranted
on more than one occasion. "Join an academic club after
school," she would say. But as long as I kept my grades up,
she indulged me.

I tried out for the swim team and just barely made it.
Over the coming weeks I worked hard to excel, just as I had
with my academics, but with lesser results. While academics came to me relatively easily, I struggled with my swimming. But I loved the challenge. That was part of the fun.

Our first meet was with our arch rival, and we hadn't
beaten them in years. When I walked out to the pool, I was
shocked to see my mother with my little sister there. My
mother had no love of sports, and hadn't warned me that
she might show up. But there she and my sister were, two
chocolate chips in a sea of vanilla ice cream.

On our marks. Get set. Then the splash of a dozen girls almost simultaneous with the explosion of the starter's pistol. We were off: four laps of an individual medley butterfly, backstroke, breaststroke, freestyle. I was predictably slow on the first three strokes. I hadn't yet really felt comfortable with them and was behind the other girls. But when we started the freestyle, I could feel a power surge in my arms and legs, and I could feel myself pulling into the competition. I didn't know where I was in relation to the other girls, but I heard the roar of the crowd and let it energize me to the finish. I had come in third. Just barely, but I was there. First was a member of our team and second was a member from our arch rival. I was quite pleased.

When I saw my mother after the event, my eyes were like Broadway klieg lights, and I clutched my third-place trophy to my breast like a favorite doll. I was beaming. I felt as if I could take on the world. My mother, however, was frowning. I don't remember the details of our fierce words, but I remember she thought that to come in third, I might as well come in last. That I would have better spent my time in academic pursuits. Tears streaming down my cheeks, I threw down the trophy and bolted away from my mother. She followed me, not uttering words of understanding or apology, but reiterating how she felt that I was wasting my time.

I dropped out of the swim team. And my mother and I never spoke about the incident again. I went on to do well in school: magna cum laude, National Honor Society, the works. Yet, there was always a hole in my soul, a bit of sadness that my mother couldn't understand and accept something that was so important to me.

Until I climbed those attic steps for the first time years later. As I sat among the boxes of photographs, my mother's wedding dress, even my crib, I reached into a box to pick up a scrapbook in which my mother had faithfully pasted the various academic and professional achievements I had been awarded over the years. I flipped through the book casually until something caught me by surprise. I stared at a yellowed clipping of my swim team victory from the local paper. I was beaming, holding my trophy high with other members of my team. And in the box where I found my scrapbook, one of maybe five filling the box, I saw something gold glinting in the butterscotch-colored sunlight that sliced through the dust particles in the musty attic. I pulled my trophy from the bottom of the box. I could still see the glue from where my mother had tried, unsuccessfully, to put my trophy back together again.

I stared at it a long time and remembered the reverberation from the announcer's voice as my name and place boomed throughout the gymnasium. When I looked up again, I saw my mother standing, gazing at me. I don't know how long she had been standing there. There was a long moment between us. And then she slowly approached, and embraced me.

AS TOLD TO ERIC V. COPAGE

EYE OF THE BEHOLDER

THE BANK TELLER sees my love's hands as things to
receive money.

Her boss sees my love's fingers as things to type
contracts.

The gym instructor sees my love's arms and shoulders
as things to be improved.

The dentist sees my love's mouth as a diary of her diet.

The department store saleswoman sees my love's scent
as a thing to be masked.

The masseuse sees my love's neck as a thing to be
loosened.

The optometrist sees my love's eyes as things to be put
behind glass.

The makeup artist sees my love's cheeks as things to be
camouflaged.

* * *

But I see magic in the flesh of my love, and reveling in
   her flesh brings me closer to her spirit.

Her hands are graceful like flags in a gentle wind.
Her fingers are long and sweet like sticks of
   cinnamon.
Her arms and shoulders are smooth and softly rounded
   like a vase.
Her mouth is an ever-blooming blossom of light.

Her scent is a zephyr that rejuvenates my soul.
Her neck graceful like the hand of a calligrapher.
Her eyes are lanterns that illuminate my heart.
Her cheeks are hills that I mount with a thousand
   kisses.

ISAAC PHILLIPS

RECIPE FOR LOVE

B ELOVED, adored, precious, treasured . . . these are some of the words that tumble forth when we think of the loves in our lives—our fathers, mothers, children, sisters, brothers, and special friends. Store-bought cards sometimes help us give voice to our deepest feelings. Some of us can conjure our own sentences. But as they say, action speaks louder than words, so be sure to season your gerunds with gestures. Here are a few possible ingredients.

1. Hug

Hugs are like multiple vitamins. But rather than *taking* one every day, be sure to *give* one every day to the ones you love. They don't always have to be bear hugs. Sometimes a slight touch on the shoulder or the elbow will do. I can hear some parents saying, "Ha! Hug my teenage son?!" I know the feeling. My son, as he approaches adolescence, looks at me with narrowing eyes if I try to embrace him in public. And I wouldn't want to embarrass him. So I slip him his hugs discreetly and in private.

2. Accept
Each of us is unique like a winter snowflake, distinct as the prints of our fingers. Revel in the individuality of your loved one, take pleasure in it! Don't try to coerce him or her to do something or act a certain way simply because it makes you happy. Also, remember that sometimes people have to make their own mistakes. So, after offering friendly, sage advice, occasionally you'll just have to watch your loved one stumble. It may be painful to witness, but just be ready to extend a loving hand after the fall.

3. Listen
There's a joke: The opposite of talking is not listening; the opposite of talking is . . . waiting for your turn to talk! How often have we been guilty of that? So remember— the opposite of talking is . . . listening! One way to check and sharpen listening skills is, at appropriate times in a conversation, to paraphrase what your loved one has said to make sure you heard it right.

4. Laugh
Yes, yes, there were years that we as a people had to "grin and bear it." And that has made some of us constitutionally adverse to smiling, afraid of being tagged a "grinning

fool," a "Tom," or worse. But the cast of your face often reflects the cast of your mind, and ultimately you are the one missing out on the splendors life has to offer by donning a frown. So come on, lighten up!

5. Share
Seen any good movies lately? Read a funny story? Notice a particularly interesting cloud formation? Share it with a loved one. However, not everything you share need be a golden moment. Let them know what annoyed you, what confused you, too. Open yourself up to your loved one. Don't be afraid.

6. Respect
One can have Technicolor disagreements with a loved one without denigrating him or her. There is no excuse to call a girlfriend a "bitch." No reason to tell a child he or she is worthless. Some people say it is good to let off steam. My own experience has been that everything in life is habit. If you get used to "letting off steam" you'll just keep on "letting off steam." It becomes a habit, and you become comfortable with it. So try taking two steps back, examining what the argument is about. It seldom happens that we get someone to change her or his mind by shouting them down, and, if done habitually, it can leave horrible emotional wreckage in its wake. Try suffocating the impulse to spew abusive language to a loved one. Try it for a week or two. See how it feels. It's just a habit.

7. Praise

When your loved one, whether it be Mom or Pop, girl-friend or baby brother, does something good, praise him or her. Whether it is tying her shoe for the first time or making that special cornbread. The first step of showing our love is looking. So let's praise our loved ones and let them know we are paying attention. Because really, what is paying attention if not love in action.

ERIC V. COPAGE

Self-Esteem

ROYALTY, PART I

IN MY CLASSES at Irvington High School, I've had
many students with low self-esteem who felt
worthless. They were usually the "shy" ones. I
would single them out to help me with projects or make
them the assistant to the substitute teacher. Also give
them honest praise: "You accomplished so much work
today—good job," or "Girl, those shoes are cute," or
"Thanks so much for your help. I couldn't have done it
without you."

One student found out that I liked Sweetarts, which
then cost just a nickel. Several times a week she would
give me some and would never take any money. "You are
so sweet," I would tell her. "You're too good to me." I
didn't give her an A or any other special treatment. She
didn't think she would get anything out of it; she was simply being nice. And I wanted to encourage that in her. I

could see her eyes brighten and watch her stand a little taller every time my positive words came her way.

Encouraging comments can do wonders for a person's self-esteem. You get him to recognize the positive things about himself that he may not have even noticed.

The older you get, the less often you're going to get that pat on the back. So you have to learn at a young age to give it to yourself. I want to make sure that the people around me, particularly my own kids and the students I teach, get that pat on the back and learn to give it to others and to themselves. That's how the cycle begins—you praise them, and they will be kind and gentle to others. You're never too old for praise.

Every year in my class, I do an exercise in which I make each student write down ten things that he or she thinks are positive about him or herself. It's amazing how many kids have never given any thought to their inner qualities. I even start them off with a few things I see in them individually. And there are a few things that I give to everyone:

1. God don't make no junk; it's that simple.
2. I was born for greatness.
3. I am beautiful in my own right.
4. I am unique, there is no one else exactly like me.
5. I can do and be anything I want.

Of course, this is high school. But adults need to embrace this philosophy, too. Sit down once in a while and examine what makes you beautiful, no matter what your age.

There is a time in everyone's life when one needs to evaluate and reevaluate oneself. You don't want to start off by beating yourself up because you haven't accomplished everything you thought you should have. It's best to start by accentuating the positive; that will help with the reevaluation process. Writing down your attributes is a way to see exactly what you have accomplished. Then you can look at where you've been and where you are and begin to figure out where you're going—and set new goals. That's why knowing yourself is so important.

RITA OWENS,
from *Ladies First*

ROYALTY, PART II

❧

BUT HOW do fear, pride, and determination make
Dana Owens a queen, you ask? And what right
does *anyone* have to call herself a queen without
sounding like one helluva arrogant sista? Well, first of all,
each of us has a queen inside. She was placed there before
we were even formed, in the womb. It's just a matter of
bringing her out. Being a woman puts you halfway there.
But there's so much more. It starts inside by feeling good
about yourself. A queen has high self-esteem. She is proud
of who she is, whether she is a corporate executive or a
cleaning lady, whether she's an athlete or a housewife.

She knows right from wrong and strives to do her best.
She doesn't player-hate or try to put other women down.
Women have a tendency to be catty or jealous of what other
women are doing or have. They will sleep with another
woman's man "just because." They will have a nasty atti-

tude toward another woman and say things like, "She thinks she's cute!" Well, that ain't cute. A real queen is so focused on keeping herself tight that she doesn't have time to be worried about the next one. A real queen is so intent on raising herself up that she can be proud of what her sisters are doing, because she's okay with herself and with God.

Queenliness is an attitude that starts on the inside and works its way out. The way you hold your head up makes you a queen. It says something about how you feel about yourself. If you walk around with your head down, you have a tendency to feel down. You are telling the world that you lack confidence, and that can signal to people that you are a target, that you will let stuff by you. It's a simple type of body language that exposes what you truly feel inside. If you're feeling down, you tend to look down. You'd be amazed at how changing your body language, lifting your head up, can give you a whole new perspective on life. You start to see things much differently, and it will begin to affect how you feel. It has to. You're no longer staring at the ground, at your problems, and not feeling good about yourself.

It's harder to feel bad with your head held high.

A queen, a woman with self-esteem, handles adversity with grace. Even when her world is crumbling around her, she never lets her crown fall. Life will put you through plenty of tests and throw many obstacles your way, but it's how you pass those tests, how you overcome those obstacles, that distinguishes you as a queen.

Think of Jacqueline Kennedy Onassis. Remember those pictures of her at President Kennedy's funeral, holding the little hands of Caroline and John-John? Just days before, she had witnessed the assassination of her children's father, her husband. She could not have felt anything but a pain too immense to put into words. Yet there she was, giving strength to the entire country. She had a pride and a will to represent something higher than herself. She was making a statement for others. She was a champion. And in many ways, she was the closest thing this country has ever had to a queen. She is remembered not for her extreme wealth and jewels, nor for her exquisite taste—although that was very much a part of who she was—but for her grace in the face of adversity, for her generosity and charity. And for always holding her head up high.

Another woman who held her head up high for the nation was, of course, Dr. Betty Shabazz. She is also a queen. As the wife of Malcolm X, she stood by a man whom many believed to be a negative force in this country. His was not a popular stance, but she was there for him. She was there when their home was firebombed. And she was in the front row at the Audubon Ballroom in Harlem when he was gunned down. She used her body to shield her four little girls, while pregnant with twins.

After her husband's tragic death, she carried on. She got her master's and doctorate and raised six girls alone. She never let anything stop her from becoming the woman she was born to be—a true American inspiration. Even after her death—in a fire set by her grandson in 1997—she remains a figure of dignity, honor, and royalty.

A queen never sells out. She will sacrifice quick money and material goods for the greater purpose of keeping her soul. She may take three jobs to take care of her two kids when Daddy's money ain't coming through, and she doesn't complain.

That was my mother, Rita Owens. She laid the foundation for me to become a self-proclaimed queen. She made the ground fertile for me to persevere, no matter what the obstacles, and to keep my head up. My mother always told me how smart, beautiful, and talented I was. In her mind, there was nothing I couldn't do. When I wanted to learn the drums and guitar, she paid for lessons. When I entered talent shows, she sat in the front row. When I played basketball, she was there, cheering the loudest. And when I got into trouble and starting running the streets, she talked with me, and she prayed for me. She never limited me. My mother believed in me before I even believed in myself. And because of that, no one can shake my confidence now. I know there are many, many young women who don't have a solid picture of what a queen is because there isn't one in their lives. But even if you don't know a strong mother—or a grandmother, a tough aunt, a straight-talking teacher, or an encouraging neighbor who can be your champion—you can still be a queen.

It starts with you. You have to want to be a queen. You have to want it for yourself. You have to know yourself.

I know who I am. I am confident. I know God. I can take care of myself. I share my life with others, and I love—I am worthy of the title Queen.

So are you.

QUEEN LATIFAH,
from *Ladies First*

LET IT BE AFRICA

❧

I T'S AN EARLY SPRING evening in Brooklyn, and
Nur Ali is moving amid the cheerful clutter of
what she calls her "mission shop," the Admiral
Family Circle, named after the Islamic collective of
which she is a part. While Mrs. Ali, fifty, calls out advice
to Ahmad, a tailor and member of the collective, she
rearranges racks of African-influenced dashikis and
bubahs, answers the intermittent ringing of a phone,
and searches through merchandise at the front of the
store in order to locate a tajj—a pillbox-shaped leather-
and-cloth hat—for her son, A. Kareem Ali Stevenson,
who takes orders for her work from his high school
classmates.

Dressed in a bubah and head wrap of African print,
Nur Ali is a modern, urban market woman, not terribly
different from her sisters in Accra or Dakar or Abidjan.

"What one African can do, another African can do," she said.

Mrs. Ali describes as "an evolution" her movement toward creating the family collective and starting the clothing business in the loft of a factory building on Atlantic Avenue. "I love the clothes, and I'm good at making them," she says. "But I don't think of this as a fashion statement; it's not about the clothes."

The evolution is as political as it is personal; at its core is a hunger, a longing for connection beyond the history of suffering and triumph that is the African-American story. It is difficult to embrace fully a history that seems to center only on loss—the loss of a homeland, of freedom, of an entire culture. But there is more to us than our arrival in the holds of alien ships, more than the challenge to the American conscience we have come to represent. We are a people who began with something greater than that mixed legacy. And from generation to generation, there have been those of us who have claimed a larger worldview, an African worldview, and joined it with our American experience.

The notion of an African-American sensibility was difficult for Nur Ali to accept. "At first I hated the whole idea," she says. "There were so many lies that were told, so many things that were done in the name of Africa that weren't real. When I was coming up, the only thing you heard about Africa was Tarzan. If somebody showed you a bunch of half-dressed people in Tarzan movies and told you that was your heritage, you'd reject it, too. But you can't misjudge Africa by the people who have misused it.

"That's the hardest thing, our next level of development: to finally become African. We can't just be black all our lives, whatever that is. The argument you always get is, 'Where in Africa?' My attitude is, first of all, let it be Africa."

ROSEMARY L. BRAY

THE KNEE-HIGH MAN
TRIES TO GET SIZABLE

❧

THE KNEE-HIGH man who lived by the swamp wanted to be big instead of little. One day he said to himself, I am going to call on the biggest thing in the neighborhood and find out how I can get sizable. So he went to see Mr. Horse. He asked, "Mr. Horse, I come to get you to tell me how to grow as big as you are."

Mr. Horse said, "Eat a whole lot of corn and then run 'round and 'round and 'round until you have gone twenty miles. After a while you will be as big as me."

So the knee-high man, he did all Mr. Horse told him to do. And the corn made his stomach hurt, and running made his legs hurt, and the trying made his mind hurt. And he just got littler and littler. Then the knee-high man sat in his house and thought about how it was that Mr. Horse didn't help him at all. And he said to himself, I'm going to see Brer Bull.

So he went to see Brer Bull and he said, "Brer Bull, I come to ask you to tell me how to get as big as you are."

And Brer Bull, he told him, "Eat a whole lot of grass and then bellow and bellow, and first thing you know you will get as big as I am."

And the knee-high man did everything that Brer Bull told him to do. And the grass made his stomach hurt, and the bellowing made his neck hurt, and the thinking made his mind hurt. And he got littler and littler. The knee-high man sat in his house and he thought about how come Brer Bull didn't do him any better than Mr. Horse. After a while, he heard old Mr. Hoot Owl in the middle of the swamp preaching that bad people are going to have bad luck. The knee-high man said to himself, I'm going to ask Mr. Hoot Owl how I can get to be sizable, and he went to see Mr. Hoot Owl.

And Mr. Hoot Owl said, "Why do you want to be big?" The knee-high man said, "I want to be big so that when I get into a fight I can win it." And Mr. Hoot Owl said, "Anybody ever try to pick a fight with you?" The knee-high man said no. So Mr. Hoot Owl said, "Well, if you don't have any cause to fight, then you don't have any reason to be bigger than you are." The knee-high man thought about that and finally said, "But I want to be big so I can see a long way." Mr. Hoot Owl, he said, "When you climb a tree, can you see a long way from the top? You know, when it comes down to it, you don't have any reason to be bigger in your body; but you sure have got a good reason to be bigger in the *brain*."

from *Afro-American Folktales*,
edited by Roger D. Abrahams

DARK-SKINDED GIRL

I'm a Dark-Skinded Girl
And oh so beautiful
My skintone is farrrrrrrrr from a curse
It's a glory
A gift
A blessing
Somethin' the world can feast its eyes upon
And marvel
That's ryt—this here skin of mine is no chore
It's not a burden—not in the least
I'm so mesmerized when I look in the mirror
Honey, sometimes I lose tract of time
'Cause I could just stand there—
Lookin'.
Studyin'.
For hours . . .

Oh, what a fool I was
I used to be so ungrateful
Oh, how I longed to be caramel or butterscotch
I'm so ashamed of my previous shame

Oh, but you should see me now

Hell, I had to cut my hair 'cause it was in the way of
    my Blackness
And it wasn't even that long

But I love my tan
I've had it 25 years now
And I wouldn't trade it for the world—
Wouldn't have it any other way
So please don't feel sorry for me when you see me
    walkin' down the street
Don't weep for me
I'm just fine
I'm having my own personal little celebration
And if you're in the way of the sun, please move—
'Cause like I said, it ain't no curse
And it ain't no chore

I've had it 25 years
And I'm gone keep on celebratin', 'cause I plan to be
    here another 70 years
And I'll be lovin' the skin I'm in
I'll be celebratin' my title as the "Dark-Skinded Girl"

AKIBA JAMA

THE JAY
AND THE PEACOCK

A JAY VENTURING into a yard where peacocks used to walk, found there a number of feathers which had fallen from the peacocks when they were moulting. He tied them all to his tail and strutted down toward the peacocks. When he came near them they soon discovered the cheat, and striding up to him pecked at him and plucked away his borrowed plumes. So the jay could do no better than go back to the other jays, who had watched his behavior from a distance; but they were equally annoyed with him, and told him: "It is not only fine feathers that make fine birds."

AESOP,
from *Aesop's Fables*

GETTING OFF
THE TREADMILL

❦

A FIVE-YEAR PLAN was not good enough for me; I devised a ten-year plan right out of college. I decided that I would strive toward my ultimate professional accomplishment to be a well-known journalist over a two-year period. If I didn't make it by that time, I would go back to school, pick up my master's in anthropology, and divide the rest of my working life between teaching at a university and doing fieldwork in Africa or Asia. I could live with that. But I wanted to go full bore for my first choice in career, and so I embarked upon my plan. First, I would get any job I could in the journalistic community, even if it involved only emptying wastepaper baskets or sharpening pencils at the local giveaway newspaper. Then, in steps lasting no more than six months each, I planned to work my way to be a practicing journalist. One who wrote for a living, no matter how meager that living might be. From there I planned to become a well-known journalist by developing my writing style and working for better and better publications. And from there, after I was on staff at a prestigious publication, I planned through writing books to distinguish myself so that my name, not just the name of the publication for which I worked, became a brand in and of itself.

My plan worked, not without a glitch here and there, but within my two-year timetable I had accomplished more than I had hoped to. I was not merely making a living as a journalist, I was a staff member at one of the best publications in the United States. I worked like a dog the next couple of years. Made contacts. My advancement seemed to slow somewhat, but I was still making progress. I was still arcing up.

Then there was a round of layoffs, and I was one of those laid off. Last hired, first fired kind of thing. But within every dark cloud there is a silver lining, and in my case the layoff was a kind of cleansing. You might even say a healing. Not off the bat, mind you, but in time I came to realize that since my graduation from college I had been ferociously focused on my career. I had no friends, only contacts. I was well read, but hadn't enjoyed a book in years. I was observant, but only of things that were of utilitarian use to me—things that might further my career.

How did I get on this treadmill, and why? In retrospect, it was in an effort to fill up a vast emptiness in myself. Some people try to fill the hollowness inside by eating, others by spending money on clothes, houses, and cars they can't afford; I channeled my feelings of worthlessness into professional accomplishments. The layoff blessed me with the opportunity to take a look at myself, at who I really was, what I really wanted. That said, I still see the opportunities I was given. And being a black person, I am dedicated to trying to position myself in life—through my position or just through the wisdom of my years—so that I might be able to help the upcoming black generation. It is important, I feel, to carry on the work of our ancestors. As a black person, I feel I have a social mission in life. But somehow I had confused the fulfillment of that social mission with empty attempts to buttress my ailing self-esteem. It is important to make sure we are trying to fulfill that social mission, but not by trying to buttress ailing self-esteem.

My company made me contract and freelance offers. And I received several staff offers from other publications, two of them competitors. So there was more than some small benefit in making contacts and doing my work exceptionally well in the past. But, seeing that I had saved some money, I decided to take time off. I went around the world for six months, and when I returned, I began dating a woman and fell in love. We are developing that relationship.

I am back at work now. I love writing and feel that through my work and simply being exposed to certain social environments—the corner offices where big decisions are made—that I can benefit black people. I can help tell them the rules of the road. But I take time to smell the roses now. I go on walks with my girlfriend, we read aloud to each other passages from novels we feel are particularly beautiful.

I know now that self-esteem—real, lasting self-esteem—doesn't come in a pay check. We are more than our work. We are relationships. We are family. It is good, even important that we blacks accomplish things in the concrete world. There is a real value in this. But I have learned that no matter how accomplished we are, no matter how rich or fawned over, the real value we find in life, the truest sense of self-esteem, comes from within.

A S   T O L D   T O   E R I C   V .   C O P A G E

THE TRUTH

❦

WHEN I COME OUT of my house, some mornings there will be old ladies sitting around there. Sometimes they wait for the mailman; sometimes they just be sitting. Well, I come out and go all the way down the line. I give each one a kiss. And you can see their faces light up like a Christmas tree. Them old ladies are sitting there and when they see me, maybe they think, "Somebody loves me." When their faces light up, my heart lights up like a Christmas tree, too.

I saw an old lady from the first floor in the hallway the other day and I said, "Hi, gorgeous." She looked so surprised. We just embraced each other and everything. She said to me, "You are so pretty." I said, "Go on, girl. You sure told the truth." I saw an old lady I know coming across the street with a girl that comes to work for her. So I came around to where I could get in front of her before she crossed the street. I said, "Hi there, young lady. Where you going?" The lady was so pleased. I might be doing it for them but how they react from me doing it makes me feel good, too. It's kind of like therapy for me.

FREDDIE MAE BAXTER,
from *The Seventh Child*

A CLOSE CALL

⚜

TELL HIM I'm not in, my new boss shouted over
his shoulder as he walked into his office. I was sitting just outside the office and had just put the
caller on hold. While the caller was listening to Monto-
vanni versions of Motown songs, I took a moment to ponder the situation. I had begun work in the company just
two days before, and in that short span my boss had asked
me to lie about his whereabouts, it seemed, dozen of times.
First it was to clients, but in the short time I had been
working with him I was asked to lie to his father and
brother. He once even had me lie to the owner of the company about his whereabouts.

It's not that I am an especially religious person—
frankly, I was more worried about the wrath of the owner
of the company if he had found out that I was lying than
the wrath of God. I know you are thinking, What rock

has this woman been living under for the past twenty-nine years? Doesn't she know that life is not columns of spit and polished soldiers marching in a straight line? Life, much of life anyway, is guerrilla warfare: springing from bushes, setting traps, and putting branches in your hair to blend in with the foliage. In other words, life can be messy, and one of the messier parts of life—for some of us anyway—is lying. I understand that I am no saint. But what my boss was asking me to do seemed gratuitous and prolific. Besides, lying just leaves a bad taste in my mouth. It's simply not the way I was brought up and I try to avoid it.

Why should I continue to make myself uncomfortable, I asked myself. Because, I answered, he is the boss. He has the power to hire, and to fire. I would be especially vulnerable this early into the job. He could just say that it wasn't working out and put me out on the street. Just like that. And jobs at this time were hard to come by. It had taken me weeks to find this one. Should I swallow my pride or speak up? Each course of action carried a potentially massive consequence.

My then-boyfriend suggested that I simply wait six months, until after I had completed my probationary period, then let him know. I considered this. But I thought it would seem too strange to comply for six months with something which I later would claim to be so upsetting. I weighed my choices overnight and awoke resolved to confront my boss with my feelings that day. I decided it was the only way I could remain whole.

In the morning, while preparing brown bag lunches

and breakfast for my two children, then age seven and nine, I wondered what I would do if my boss should take offense. Certainly I would be out of a job. But my father was at the end of his financial rope, so he wouldn't be able to help, and so was my boyfriend. Neither could be counted on to loan me money for the period of time it might take to find a new job. Besides, it would just be a loan and I would just be getting into debt. Last, once they learned why I lost my job, they might not loan me money out of sheer principle. You lost the job you sought for weeks because of what!? I imagined them exclaiming. No, here I was on my own.

I kissed the children good-bye and put them on the school bus, and then drove to the office, my heart beating hard beneath my ribs. It was as if I were running a marathon, although my only exertion was moving my right foot from the gas pedal to the brake pedal.

When I reached the office, I sat at my desk with the sinking feeling I imagine a death row prisoner has waiting for the hour of his execution. When the phone rang, I picked it up, hoping for the love of God my boss wouldn't ask me to lie at that moment—the moment before telling him I wasn't going to take it anymore. He arrived forty-five minutes later than usual. "Traffic," he said, taking the clutch of messages I held out for him. Then he disappeared into his office. I followed him in.

"Excuse me," I said, trying to lower the register of my voice so that I wouldn't sound scared. "I have to talk to you about something."

He was standing at his desk, but hadn't yet sat down. He

was a short man, a potbelly made him look like an oval, and he had thinning brown hair that had not a trace of gray in it yet. He was studying something on his calendar and when he heard me, he didn't move except to peer up at me with his gray-green eyes. He nodded quickly and, it seemed, impatiently.

"It's about your whereabouts," I said. "I simply can't keep lying about it. It's simply not the way I grew up and I feel uncomfortable about it." I was about to say that I simply wouldn't do it, but held back. Why make this any more confrontational than it was?

He sat down. Here, it's coming, I thought. Back to the unemployment office, back to the help wanted ads in the daily paper. Back to budgeting to the penny, rather than budgeting to the quarter, a luxury this job gave me.

He put his fingertips together and said, "I understand." And went on to say that he admired me for speaking up. "But," he said, "we have a practical problem."

He told me that he was in the throes of a messy divorce and that his soon-to-be ex-wife—or more specifically her lawyer—was throwing curveballs at him at every opportunity, forms and figures that had to be filled out and returned within a limited period of time.

So he concluded, "I have been trying to put as much of work, except for critical matters, on the back burner. That is why I have been avoiding calls. It won't be this bad forever. But the larger question is, what can you tell people, even after my divorce is over, that you'll be comfortable with when I can't or don't want to take a call."

He and I tried out several ideas. Being unavailable was

true, but too enigmatic. We decided to say he was in a meeting, since when he was talking with his lawyer he most certainly was in a meeting, and when he was reading correspondence, no matter from whom, it constituted a kind of meeting. I felt in the clear conscience-wise. And I was not disgracing my upbringing, nor my self-esteem.

AS TOLD TO ERIC V. COPAGE

WHEN WORDS ARE ENOUGH

~~~✦~~~

A MONG THE BLACK WOMEN posse at school—
Angie, Karen, Valerie, and me—there was a strong
sisterhood that I hadn't had since my double-dutch
days. I started spending time in the "mod" townhouse
where these girls lived. They were sophomores and their
housing was a step above my freshman dorm. Hanging out
with them, I used vocabulary that I had always felt afraid
to use at home. Angie, Karen, and Valerie were special
because they were each top students but they could also get
down. They laughed at me for being stiff, but they also
made me feel comfortable.

Back home, I had always felt too shy to dance. Every
black party was like a mini episode of *Soul Train*—boys
and girls looking good and shaking their groove thang.
The dances that filtered through New York to Atlanta to
Chicago to Los Angeles and back around again came and

went so quickly. By the time I learned a dance it was on its way out. Every party was cause for scrutiny and even if I attempted a new dance in the corner where nobody was looking, some bigmouth was sure to say "Oooh, girl, check it out. Veronica is getting down with the wop." Then I'd get embarrassed and stop.

Simon's Rock dances were a joke, as I learned during the orientation week "jam." First of all, you spent the better part of the evening convincing the so-called DJ to play some up-to-date rap music, not just the Run-DMC cover of Aerosmith's "Walk This Way." Then, once the tunes started bumping, there was no way any dance you did could be wrong. It seemed like the white students were dancing to completely different music. The long-haired, hippie-girl "modern" dancers actually twirled their skirts and made shapes during Hammer's "Can't Touch This." Other kids slam-danced to everything from Madonna to Young MC.

I would call my mother and describe this scene to her. I made the stories elaborate and colorful and I loved to hear her voice laughing on the phone. When I told her about how the white kids were slam-dancing to Bob Marley's "No Woman, No Cry," we both laughed so hard I thought we'd never stop.

When I hung out with Angie, Karen, and Valerie, I loved the way we addressed each other: it was always "girlfriend," "sis," "flygirl." We punctuated our stories with "Chile, please" and "Honey, let me tell you." It made me remember that I was the girl who had stomped around Beverly Road answering the call of "Oooh, she thinks

she's fine" with a resounding "Baby, I *know* I'm fine."
When girls like the ones in L.A. and Brooklyn stepped to
me and wanted to fight, I never felt the need to speak their
language. I never saw myself in them. But I saw myself in
Angie, Karen, and Valerie. As isolated as we were at
Simon's Rock, the language became a way of plugging us
back into our hometowns. The words were warm and
comfortable, like connectors to the darkest and most beautiful parts of myself, and when I reached out to them, I
felt electric and alive.

VERONICA CHAMBERS,
from *Mama's Girl*

MY OWN TWO FEET

❧❧❧

Four events of great personal importance happened to me in 1945. All efforts to maintain the marriage with Frankie Dee Brown came to an end. I came to a new level of myself as a woman. Franklin Delano Roosevelt died. And I worked with an actor I had never heard of before—Ossie Davis.

Frankie was a sincere and decent person, and a good provider, but marriage to him was becoming more and more unsatisfactory. During this time, he would occasionally stalk me. At rehearsal, people would tell me they had run into him and that he was not friendly, that he was angry and waiting for me outside. I began to be afraid of him.

Early in 1945, I asked him for a divorce, and finally he agreed, saying he would attend to the legalities. I still stayed at the house, however, when he was away, but I went to Mother's when he was due back in town.

Back and forth between Frank's house and my mother's apartment, I was uncertain of how to go about initiating the divorce. He'd done nothing about it. I suppose I should have just made a clean break, but I liked being in the old brownstone when he wasn't there—the privacy of living alone, despite Frankie's father who stayed on the ground floor. Besides, we hadn't yet made arrangements, or discussed who would take care of the house, handle the expenses, the bills, and so forth. I couldn't just turn my back and walk away.

When it was known that we were separated, men began to look at me differently and I even received two marriage proposals. I guess I exuded an air of availability. It was a heady, scary time. I had never experienced this kind of attention before and I welcomed it.

I began to date a Harlem businessman, who soon had me spinning like a top. He seemed so knowledgeable and self-confident, and gave me a sense of security and strength. He had broad, comfortable shoulders, was gentle and reassuring, and made me feel as if I were the only woman in the world possible for him. He had taken me many places, including two business meetings, at one of which I waited for him for two hours. He spoke affectionately, but for a long time he had not even tried to kiss me. All that was to change.

One beautiful day, we sailed up the Hudson River. I'd never been on a yacht before. After a light meal, he took me to the quarters below deck, and after a while, he proceeded to undress me, to kiss me, and to tell me of his love. He then carried me to a small but elegant bathroom, put me in a bubble bath he'd prepared, washed, dried, then wrapped me in a towel that looked like clouds, and carried me to an exquisitely dressed bed.

Before he returned from his bath, I looked around at the luxurious, cozy setting, felt the motion of the boat, and listened to the soft music as it accompanied the sound of the water. Paradise, I thought, must be something like this. With my friend that day, I experienced more about the physical aspects of love, about suspense, sensuality, and excitement than I'd even imagined. What a marvelous lover! Could anything on earth or heaven compare with the joy of this experience?

He had "located all the bells and blown all the whistles," was how my sister LaVerne expressed it after he dropped me at her apartment on One Hundred Fiftieth Street, where I spent the night. I told her what had happened. We both concluded that I must be in love.

We met frequently at his apartment, and after about a month, he gave me the keys. I don't remember discussing love, marriage, or relationship issues. I felt I was on a roller coaster in an adult amusement park. His attention was constant and almost overwhelming. He made me feel that I belonged to him completely, like an obsession.

One day, we had arranged to meet at his place, but I was early and intended to let myself in as usual and wait. The keys, to my consternation, didn't work, because the door was bolted from the inside. A kind of panic began as I called for him to let me in. It seemed to start from the base of my spine and work itself up to my head and through my mouth as I continued to call and bang on the door. He was inside with someone! I could hear voices, muffled voices, women's voices, whispering, scuffling, and scurrying around. What was going on in there?

How dare he invite me to his house and lock the door against me? Who the hell did he—? What the hell—? "Let me in before I break down this door!" I screamed, pounded, and kicked the door. Never had I felt such fury. I knew they heard me. The world probably heard me.

Dogs. Dogs. Men are just dogs! My mother is right. You are all dogs! With shoulders, hips, fists, I tried to break the very substantial door. I had to get in. All hell was not going to keep me out!

Finally, I heard the floor bolt being moved. Locks unlocked, and a sheepish-looking man, my friend's driver, opened the door. My anger blazed past him to two women who seemed in shock as I slammed my way into the apartment, feeling blood and fire pumping from every aperture in my body. *He* wasn't there!

The driver then explained that he had been instructed to call and inform me that a sudden trip out of town had been necessary and that my friend could not keep our date—but he had completely forgotten to tell me. As the two young women, who seemed to have dressed hurriedly, sat in the living room looking embarrassed, the driver apologized profusely and asked if I would see fit not to report the incident.

I fled the scene, trembling, a cold escape in a sweaty body, trying to recover from a sickening, jealous rage. My hand hurt from all the pounding, and my mind hurt to think that this angry, irrational, dangerous person of a few minutes ago could be me!

Through that experience, I discovered dimensions of myself I had never known. The bursting forth from girlhood into womanhood was painful, but in retrospect, it was beautiful, too. It taught me how little and how much it means to be a sexually fulfilled woman. I was no longer spinning like a top. I had reclaimed myself and was standing on my own two feet.

My friend continued to travel a great deal, but it didn't matter now. When I looked at him, he was the same man—confident, charming, debonair—but something in me had changed. With so much happening in my personal life and in the political life of this country, before I could take stock, he had traveled out of my mind.

RUBY DEE,
from *With Ossie and Ruby*

RECIPE FOR SELF-ESTEEM

❧

O VER THE PAST two decades or so, volumes have been devoted to "self-esteem": where to find it, how to get it, where to put it once you lock your eager arms around it. But when I was a child in the early sixties, no one ever talked to me or my contemporaries about self-esteem. Brushing and bathing and a clean pair of drawers seemed to take care of the matter on a physical level. In the metaphysical realm, the knowledge that God loves each and every one of us seemed to suffice. Everyday feelings of social redemption were a bit trickier, but still there was a simple and remarkably effective solution. The assumption was that if you did well—whether it be in school or at work or on the playground—you would feel good. You would be imbued with self-esteem, regardless of how others saw you. Therefore, the efforts of our parents, grandparents, and teachers were directed toward impressing upon us that we were capable of doing anything our little hearts desired. Our elders didn't hector us or lecture us; they didn't set us adrift with a boatload of platitudes. They gave us compass and sextant—showed us the habits that would lead to success, knowing that success leads to self-esteem. (Though they also had something to say about those who pursued success to the exclusion of everything else.) Here are a few of their tips:

1. Breathe
This sounds obvious, but you'd be amazed at how few people do it. I'm not talking about shallow, upper chest breathing. I mean deep breathing that comes from the diaphragm, a breath that seems to expand your belly as you inhale. Why is deep breathing so important? Because a deep breath helps you relax, and relaxation is the key to restoration of body, mind, and spirit. Deep breathing makes you more alert and responsive to the world around you.

2. Slow It Down
Think about what you want to do before you do it especially if it is an unfamiliar task. Take your time. Don't rush.

3. Break It Up
Don't bite off more than you can chew. If you have something to do, break it down into smaller parts. Trying to learn a difficult song? Tackle it measure by measure. Uncertain about how to get that promotion? Think about

the elements of the path you must take to get there, and work on each of them one at a time. Wondering how to get a better grade in a subject in school? Take apart the problem to get a thorough understanding of it.

4. Visualize

Vivid visualization has always been one of the most important success aids. It is most effective to visualize the end result. So if you want that job—in addition to the real-world preparations of getting it—lay down, relax, and see the door with your name on it, see yourself walking confidently down the halls of the establishment. See yourself being congratulated for a job well done. Ogle the many digits in your plump checking and savings accounts.

5. Practice, Man, Practice

There is an old joke: On a New York street corner, one guy asks another, "How do you get to Carnegie Hall?" Without a beat comes the reply: "Practice, man, practice." That is sage advice for any endeavor. And the most effective practice will involve incorporating the first four success tips into your practice routines.

ERIC V. COPAGE

Family

BROTHERS

We're related—you and I,
You from the West Indies,
I from Kentucky.

Kinsmen—you and I,
You from Africa,
I from the U.S.A.

Brothers—you and I.

LANGSTON HUGHES

COFFEE SIGNS

❦

MY GRANDPARENTS lived on Mulvaney Street in Knoxville. For the longest time I sang, "Here we go 'round the mulvaney bush," being quite sure at that young age that others were mispronouncing. Is it that things seem so much better with age or from a distance? I'm sure I was bored many an evening as we three sat on the front porch watching the JFG COFFEE sign flick on and off . . . on and off. Yet it is a peaceful memory. I loved the sound of the train whistle. It always seemed to bring rain. Logic says the whistle blew at other times, and in any rational system I would know that it was only on rainy days that I was in the house to hear it. Yet even now a train whistle brings the smell of rain to me, the dark clouds, flashes of lightning, and the warmth of sitting in the living room listening to Grandpapa tell stories until the storm had passed. Nothing is learned until the spirit incorporates it; nothing has passed until it is forgotten. Knoxville and I may change, should change, but there will always be, for me, that porch, facing the tennis courts of Cal Johnson Park and, at a forty-five-degree angle, the lights of JFG COFFEE flicking on and off . . . on and off . . . and the two people with whom I sat.

NIKKI GIOVANNI,
from *Racism 101*

EVERYONE'S CHILD

IF ONE'S REPUTATION is a possession, then of all my possessions, my reputation means most to me. Nothing comes even close to it in importance. Now and then, I have wondered whether my reputation matters too much to me; but I can no more easily renounce my concern with what other people think of me than I can will myself to stop breathing. No matter what I do, or where or when I do it, I feel the eyes of others on me, judging me.

Who is watchin' me? The living and the dead. My father is watching me. My father, whose mouth dropped open when he first saw Jeanne, my wife. She looked so much like my mother, he said. He is still a force in my life. Some years ago, before he died of a stroke in 1989, I was being interviewed by the television journalist Charlayne Hunter-Gault in her home.

"Tell me, Arthur," she said, laughter in her voice, "how

is it that I have never heard anyone say anything bad about you? How is it that you have never cursed an umpire, or punched an opponent, or gotten a little drunk and disorderly? Why are you such a goody-goody?"

I laughed in turn, and told the truth.

"I guess I have never misbehaved because I'm afraid that if I did anything like that, my father would come straight up from Virginia, find me wherever I happen to be, and kick my ass." When I told that story not long ago on Men's Day at the Westwood Baptist Church in Richmond, Virginia, everyone smiled and some folks even laughed. They knew what I was talking about, even those few living in that little enclave of blacks surrounded by whites in Richmond who had never met my father. They knew fathers (and mothers) exactly like him, who in times past would come up and find you wherever you were and remind you exactly who you were and don't you forget it. You were their child, that's who.

ARTHUR ASHE,
from *Days of Grace*

AN UPHILL CLIMB

❧

WHAT MADE OUR LIVES WORK as well as they did was my mother's genius at making do—worn into her by a childhood of rural poverty—along with her vivid imagination. She worked at home endlessly, shopped ruthlessly, bargained, cajoled, charmed. Her food store of choice was the one that stocked pork and beans, creamed corn, sardines, Vienna sausages, and potted meat all at ten cents a can. Clothing was the stuff of rummage sales, trips to Goodwill and bargain basements, where thin cotton and polyester reigned supreme. Our shoes came from a discount store that sold two pairs for five dollars.

It was an uphill climb, but there was no time for reflection; we were too busy with our everyday lives. Yet I remember how much it pained me to know that Mama, who recruited a neighbor to help her teach me how to read when I was three, found herself left behind by her eldest daughter, then by each of us in turn. Her biggest worry was that we would grow up uneducated, so Mama enrolled us in parochial school.

When one caseworker angrily questioned how she could afford to send four children to St. Ambrose School, my mother, who emphatically declared, "My kids need an education," told her it was none of her business. (In fact, the school had a volume discount of sorts; the price of tuition dropped with each child you sent. I still don't know quite how she managed it.) She organized our lives around church and school, including Mass every morning at 7:45. My brother was an altar boy; I laid out the vestments each afternoon for the next day's Mass. She volunteered as a chaperone for every class trip, sat with us as we did home- work she did not understand herself. She and my father reminded us again and again and again that every book, every test, every page of homework was in fact a ticket out and away from the life we lived.

ROSEMARY L. BRAY,
from *Unafraid of the Dark*

A VOTE OF CONFIDENCE

I WAS SCANNING the course listings when I spotted a talismanic name: Erika Fromm. I assumed this Fromm to be the daughter of the famous psychoanalyst and author, Erich Fromm, who'd been a student of Freud's. Dr. Fromm was teaching The Psychology of the Ego, the only course on the menu that required "an interview with the professor."

The woman who met me at the office door looked to be in her sixties, old enough to be venerable, old enough perhaps to have known Freud himself. She had a Valkyrie's high cheekbones and her hair was swept up and back from her face, in wings. She took her place in the leather armchair and motioned for me to sit in the plain wooden chair that faced it.

"You vish to study vis me ze psychology of the ego?"

I did.

"Do you know vat ego psychology iss?"

Yes, I said. I did. And I did. I tried to speak, but she cut me off, then lectured me about Anna Freud's breakthroughs in ego psychology. Before long, I was drunk on those apple-size cheekbones, and especially on what I thought was a Viennese accent, the way she said zis, zees, zose, and zat.

"I vill admit you," she said.

Nothing could have prepared me for what she said next: "Vee haff been horrible to ze bleck people, we haff treated zem so badly. Vee haff to make it up. It may take you a lit-tle longer to get ze degree, but you vill get it."

We have to make it up. . . . It may take you longer to get your degree . . . but you will get it.

I was numb. It seemed Erika had told me that I was a dull child, to be treated with pity and patience, that I should accept her condolences in advance for the difficulty I would have. The best I could do was nod until I got my senses back.

Back at my hotel, I went over my documents. The tran-script said "dean's list, dean's list, dean's list." It said Alpha Chi National Scholarship Honor Society. It said cum laude graduate, and I cursed myself for falling six one-hundredths of a percentage point short of magna cum laude. I read again the wilted clipping from *The Delaware County Daily Times:* "Brent A. Staples, son of Mr. And Mrs. Melvin Staples, 316 Ward St., Chester, has won a Danforth Fellowship for advanced study for the Ph.D. degree. . . . A frequent dean's list student throughout his four years at college, he was elected president of his fresh-man class . . ." Nowhere did the story say that I was a foundling who'd gotten into college by accident. But it came close: ". . . Staples enrolled at Widener as 1 of 23 'academic risks' in the Project Prepare program for educationally disadvantaged students." There it was again: "risk." I wondered if I'd ever be shed of it.

I needed a vote of confidence. I got it from one of the secretaries in the psychology department, a bosomy, brown-skinned woman with a warming smile. Her name was Deloise and I applied to her for office space. She produced a ring of keys and told me to follow her. We got off the elevator on the second floor and stopped one door short of Erika Fromm's office. Deloise threw open the door and said, "This is it. You can have this one." The office was vast, the same size as Frau Dr. Fromm's. The window was framed in ivy and overlooked the green tranquility of the social science quadrangle. Mine was not the customary arrangement. Students just down the hall were crammed three to an office: three desks, three sets of books, three coffee cups, always one with fungus growing in it.

Brown-skinned Providence smiled upon me from every corner of the campus. Secretaries seemed to beam when I came into the room. At the housing office, they helped me find a cheap apartment across the Midway at the edge of Woodlawn. Five sunny rooms, with a sun porch and a walk-in pantry.

BRENT STAPLES,
from *Parallel Time*

THE ABCs OF KIN

A Member of Your Family . . .

A-llows you to be yourself.

B-rings out the best in you.

C-ommands your respect by what she does, not only by
what she says.

D-oesn't draw conclusions about you based on hearsay.

E-njoys your company.

F-ills you with love, hope, and happiness.

G-uards your privacy.

H-elps you no matter what.

I-s anybody you choose it to be.

J-olts you back to reality when you need it.

K-eeps his promises.

L-aughs with you.

M-isses you.

N-otices changes you've made.

O-pens you up to new things.

P-rays for you, but never preaches at you.

Q-uestions you when appropriate.

R-eceives your unconditional love and affection.

S-hakes you up when you need to be shaken.

T-oasts to the strength of your relationship.

U-rges you to do your best.

V-isits you.

W-ants the best for you.

X-tends a tender, helping hand.

Y-ields to her highest impulses, and embraces yours.

Z-eroes in on your relationship.

ERIC V. COPAGE

THE ULTIMATE GIFT

FOR MY FATHER'S funeral I had nothing black to wear and this posed a nagging problem all day long. It was one of those problems, simple, or impossible of solution, to which the mind insanely clings in order to avoid the mind's real trouble. I spent most of that day at the downtown apartment of a girl I knew, celebrating my birthday with whiskey and wondering what to wear that night. When planning a birthday celebration one naturally does not expect that it will be up against competition from a funeral and this girl had anticipated taking me out that night, for a big dinner and a night club afterward. Sometime during the course of that long day we decided that we would go out anyway, when my father's funeral service was over. I imagine *I* decided it, since, as the funeral hour approached, it became clearer and clearer to me that I would not know what to do with myself when it was over. The girl, stifling her very lively concern as to the possible effects of the whiskey on one of my father's chief mourners, concentrated on being conciliatory and practically helpful. She found a black shirt for me somewhere and ironed it and, dressed in the darkest pants and jacket I owned, and slightly drunk, I made my way to my father's funeral.

The chapel was full, but not packed, and very quiet. There were, mainly, my father's relatives and his children, and here and there I saw faces I had not seen since childhood, the faces of my father's onetime friends. They were very dark and solemn now, seeming somehow to suggest that they had known all along that something like this would happen. Chief among the mourners was my aunt, who had quarreled with my father all his life; by which I do not mean to suggest that her mourning was insincere or that she had not loved him. I suppose that she was one of the few people in the world who had, and their incessant quarreling proved precisely the strength of the tie that bound them. The only other person in the world, as far as I knew, whose relationship to my father rivaled my aunt's in depth was my mother, who was not there.

It seemed to me, of course, that it was a very long funeral. But it was, if anything, a rather shorter funeral than most, nor, since there were no overwhelming, uncontrollable expressions of grief, could it be called—if I dare to use the word—successful. The minister who preached my father's funeral sermon was one of the few my father had still been seeing as he neared his end. He presented to us in his sermon a man whom none of us had ever seen—

a man thoughtful, patient, and forbearing, a Christian inspiration to all who knew him, and a model for his children. And no doubt the children, in their disturbed and guilty state, were almost ready to believe this; he had been remote enough to be anything and, anyway, the shock of the incontrovertible, that it was really our father lying up there in that casket, prepared the mind for anything. His sister moaned and this grief-stricken moaning was taken as corroboration. The other faces held a dark, noncommittal thoughtfulness. This was not the man they had known, but they had scarcely expected to be confronted with *him;* this was, in a sense deeper than questions of fact, the man they had not known, and the man they had not known may have been the real one. The real man, whoever he had been, had suffered and now he was dead: this was all that was sure and all that mattered now. Every man in the chapel hoped that when his hour came he, too, would be eulogized, which is to say forgiven, and that all of his lapses, greeds, errors, and strayings from the truth would be invested with coherence and looked upon with charity. This was perhaps the last thing human beings could give each other and it was what they demanded, after all, of the Lord. Only the Lord saw the midnight tears, only He was present when one of His children, moaning and wringing hands, paced up and down the room. When one slapped one's child in anger the recoil in the heart reverberated through heaven and became part of the pain of the universe. And when the children were hungry and sullen and distrustful and one watched them, daily, growing wilder, and further away, and running headlong into danger, it was the Lord who knew what the charged heart endured as the strap was laid to the backside; the Lord alone who knew what one *would* have said if one had had, like the Lord, the gift of the living word. It was the Lord who knew of the impossibility every parent in that room faced: how to prepare the child for the day when the child would be despised and how to *create* in the child—by what means?—a stronger antidote to this poison than one had found for oneself. The avenues, side streets, bars, billiard halls, hospitals, police stations, and even the playgrounds of Harlem—not to mention the houses of correction, the jails, and the morgue—testified to the potency of the poison while remaining silent as to the efficacy of whatever antidote, irresistibly raising the worse, the question of whether or not an antidote was desirable; perhaps poison should be fought with poison. With these several schisms in the mind and with more terrors in the heart than could be named, it was better not to judge the man who had gone down under an impossible burden. It was better to remember: *Thou knowest this man's fall; but thou knowest not his wrassling.*

While the preacher talked and I watched the children—years of changing their diapers, scrubbing them, slapping them, taking them to school, and scolding them had had the perhaps inevitable result of making me love them, though I am not sure I knew this then—my mind was busily breaking out with a rash of disconnected impressions. Snatches of popular songs, indecent jokes, bits of books I had read, movie sequences, faces, voices, political issues—I thought I was going mad; all these impressions suspended, as it were, in the solution of the faint nausea produced in me by the heat and liquor. For a moment I had the impression that my alcoholic breath, inefficiently disguised with chewing gum, filled the entire chapel. Then someone began singing one of my father's favorite songs and, abruptly, I was with him, sitting on his knee, in the hot, enormous, crowded church which was the first church we attended. It was the Abyssinian Baptist Church of One Hundred Thirty-eighth Street. We had not gone there long. With this image, a host of others came. I had forgotten, in the rage of my growing up, how proud my father had been of me when I was little. Apparently, I had had a voice and my father had liked to show me off before the members of the church. I had forgotten what he had looked like when he was pleased but now I remembered that he had always been grinning with pleasure when my solos ended. I even remembered certain expressions on his face when he teased my mother—had he loved her? I would never know. And when had it all begun to change? For now it seemed that he had not always been cruel. I remembered being taken for a haircut and scraping my knee on the footrest of the barber's chair and I remembered my father's face as he soothed my crying and applied the stinging iodine. Then I remembered our fights, fights which had been of the worst possible kind because my technique had been silence.

I remembered the one time in all our life together when we had really spoken to each other.

It was on a Sunday and it must have been shortly before

I left home. We were walking, just the two of us, in our usual silence, to or from church. I was in high school and had been doing a lot of writing and I was, at about this time, the editor of the high school magazine. But I had also been a Young Minister and had been preaching from the pulpit. Lately, I had been taking fewer engagements and preached as rarely as possible. It was said in the church, quite truthfully, that I was "cooling off."

My father asked me abruptly, "You'd rather write than preach, wouldn't you?"

I was astonished at his question—because it was a real question. I answered, "Yes."

That was all we said. It was awful to remember that that was all we had *ever* said.

The casket now was opened and the mourners were being led up the aisle to look for the last time on the deceased. The assumption was that the family was too overcome with grief to be allowed to make this journey alone and I watched while my aunt was led to the casket and, muffled in black and shaking, led back to her seat. I disapproved of forcing the children to look on their dead father, considering that the shock of his death, or, more truthfully, the shock of death as a reality, was already a little more than a child could bear, but my judgment in this matter had been overruled and there they were, bewildered and frightened and very small, being led, one by one, to the casket. But there is also something very galant about children at such moments. It has something to do with their silence and gravity and with the fact that one cannot help them. Their legs, somehow, seem *exposed,* so that it is at once incredible and terribly clear that their legs are all they have to hold them up.

I had not wanted to go to the casket myself and I certainly had not wished to be led there, but there was no way of avoiding either of these forms. One of the deacons led me up and I looked on my father's face. I cannot say that it looked like him at all. His blackness had been equivocated by powder and there was no suggestion in that casket of what his power had or could have been. He was simply an old man dead, and it was hard to believe that he had ever given anyone either joy or pain. Yet, his life filled that room. Further up the avenue his wife was holding his newborn child. Life and death so close together, and love and hatred, and right and wrong, said something to me which I did not want to hear concerning man, concerning the life of man.

JAMES BALDWIN,
from *Notes of a Native Son*

FAMILY OF THE HEART

❦

THREE YEARS AGO I became so depressed I couldn't sleep. I couldn't eat. And in just over a week I went from being a nonsmoker to inhaling over two packs a day. Other than going to work—where I felt like I was walking though Jell-O—I was a virtual hermit in my house.

The first person I told was my mother, and over the phone I could hear the terror in her voice. It was my first major crisis away from my parents. And when I told my father, he told me to come home. But I felt that returning to my family, as loving as that family had been and continues to be, wasn't the right move. When the plane hit the tarmac eight hundred miles away, I would again be their daughter, and their first instinct would be to hold and protect their daughter. That would have been a regression from which I was afraid I would never emerge.

Then my other family stepped in. My family of the heart. They had noticed that I had retreated, that I was walking through life unable to cry or laugh, and began circling around me to come to the rescue. They had known me as an adult, and could see my strength through the weakness.

My friend Faye, whom I had known for twelve years, badgered me into getting out of my self-imposed exile. As we sat at an Atlanta cafe, she tried to get some emotional response from me—anger, sadness, anything. But nothing came. I can remember her eyes brimming with tears, tears that I wasn't able to shed.

Jean, a brilliant neuropsychologist whom I had known for five years, threatened to fly in from Boston and physically take me to the doctor. And I knew that she would, so her threat helped me along the path to recovery.

Walking with me around a high school track was my friend Docc's specialty. He was a neighbor, and during our promenades he would let me talk or, equally important, not talk. He would make me laugh, and it was then that I knew I was getting better.

Today I am healing. I can breathe again—without the benefit of cigarettes. I am a mental health activist. And my friendship with Docc has blossomed, so that I have been able to reclaim love. My family of the heart taught me a huge lesson: Trust. My illness was a humbling confrontation with my need for other people. It has made me a gentler person. It has made me wiser. And I have to thank for all of that my family of the heart.

VANESSA JACKSON

UNDERGROUND DADS

※

FOR YEARS, while growing up, I shamelessly told my playmates that I didn't have a father. In my neighborhood, where men went to work with lunch pails, my friends thought there was a gaping hole in my household. My father never came to the park with me to toss a softball, never came to see me in any of my school plays. I'd explain to friends, with the simplicity of explaining to someone that there are, in some woods, no deer, that I just had no father. My friends looked at me and squinted.

My mother and father had divorced shortly after my birth. As the years rolled by, however, I did not have the chance to turn into the pitiful little black boy who had been abandoned by his father. There was a reason: other men showed up. They were warm, honest (at least as far as my eyes could see), and big-hearted. They were the good black men in the shadows, the men who taught me right from wrong, who taught me how to behave, who told me, by their very actions, that they expected me to do good things in life.

There are heartbreaking statistics tossed about regarding single-parent black households these days, about children growing up fatherless. Those statistics must be considered. But how do you count the other men, the ones who show up—with perfect timing, with a kind of soft-stepping loveliness—to give a hand, to take a boy to watch airplanes lift off, to show a young boy the beauty of planting tomatoes in the ground, and to tell a child that all of life is not misery?

In my life, there was Jerry, who hauled junk. He had a lean body and a sweet smile. He walked like a cowboy, all bowlegged, swinging his shoulders. It was almost a strut. The sound of his pickup truck rumbling down our alley in Columbus, Ohio, could raise me from sleep.

When he wasn't hauling junk, Jerry fixed things. More than once, he fixed my red bicycle. The gears were always slipping; the chain could turn into a tangled mess. Hearing pain in my voice, Jerry would instruct me to leave my bike on our front porch. In our neighborhood, in the sixties, no one would steal your bike from your porch. Jerry promised me he'd pick it up, and he always did. He never lied to me, and he cautioned me not to tell lies. He was, off and on, my mother's boyfriend. At raucous family gatherings, he'd pull me aside and explain to me the importance of honesty, of doing what one promised to do.

And there was Jimmy, my grandfather, who all his life

paid his bills the day they arrived: That was a mighty lesson in itself—it taught me a work ethic. He held two jobs, and there were times when he allowed me to accompany him on his night job, where he cleaned a Greek restaurant on the north side of Columbus. Often he'd mop the place twice, as if trying to win some award. He frightened me, too. It was not because he was mean. It was because he had exacting standards, and there were times when I didn't measure up to those standards. He didn't like shortcutters. His instructions, on anything, were to be carried out to the letter. He believed in independence, doing as much for yourself as you possibly could. It should not have surprised me when, one morning while having stomach pains, he chose not to wait for a taxi and instead walked the mile to the local hospital, where he died a week later of stomach cancer.

My uncles provided plenty of good background music when I was coming of age. Uncle Henry took me fishing. He'd phone the night before: "Be ready, seven o'clock." I'd trail him through woods—as a son does a father—until we found our fishing hole. We'd sit for hours. He taught me patience and an appreciation of the outdoors, of nature. He talked incessantly, of family—his family, my family, the family of friends. The man had a reverence for family. I knew to listen.

I think these underground fathers simply appear, decade to decade, flowing through the generations. Hardly everywhere, and hardly, to be sure, in enough places, but there. As mystical, sometimes, as fate when fate is sweet.

Sometimes I think that all these men who have swept

in and out of my life still couldn't replace a good, warm father. But inasmuch as I've never known a good, warm father, the men who entered my life, who taught me right from wrong, who did things they were not asked to do, have become unforgettable. I know of the cold statistics out there. And yet, the mountain of father-son literature does not haunt me. I've known good black men.

WIL HAYGOOD

THE LION
AND THE MOUSE

✦

ONCE when a lion was asleep a little mouse began running up and down upon him; this soon wakened the
lion, who placed his huge paw upon him, and opened
his big jaws to swallow him. "Pardon, O king," cried the little
mouse, "forgive me this time, I shall never forget it: Who knows
but what I may be able to do you a turn some of these days?"
The lion was so tickled at the idea of the mouse being able to
help him that he lifted up his paw and let him go. Some time
after the lion was caught in a trap, and the hunters who desired
to carry him alive to the king tied him to a tree while they went
in search of a wagon to carry him on. Just then the little mouse
happened to pass by and, seeing the sad plight the lion was in,
went up to him and soon gnawed away the ropes that bound the
king of the beasts. "Was I not right?" said the little mouse.

Little friends may prove great friends.

A E S O P , from *Aesop's Fables*

AN UNMARKED MAN

I N A G E S T U R E oddly ancient, a young man's chest
was offered for tribal marking. He stood on his knees,
bare from the waist up. His irregular breathing spoke
fear in an arrhythmic cadence of grunts and sucking air.

I watched as he threw back his head, bracing for the
burning touch. His "brothers" held him as steady as they
could, chanting in deep ragged voices. A smell much like
that of frying bacon soon hung heavy in the morning air.

I was in a mobile home moored at the edge of More-
head State University in eastern Kentucky some twenty
years ago. I had earned my place there. After months of
pledging and enduring a battery of physical and psychological tests, I had proved my worthiness for joining
Omega Psi Phi Fraternity.

While pledging, I had, along with my brothers, exhib-
ited selflessness, determination, and grit. I had been bat-
tered with oarlike paddles; I had recited fraternity lore as

matches flared between my fingers, and most of the time
I had slept little and eaten even less while preserving my
B-plus average and some modicum of dignity. For many
years afterward, whenever I was about to face a difficult
challenge, I would remind myself that it could not be as
hard as pledging.

I had also learned that brotherhood need not be a consequence of common parentage and a shared sex. Something precious and delicate was forged among eight very
different teenagers from eight very different places and
experiences.

And so I stood in a darkened living room the width of a
one-car garage, proud to become an Omega man. The others I had pledged with were also entering the fraternity
that day and, one by one, were being branded with the
mark of their new tribe.

Even today, I feel a great deal in common with every
man who knows our secret handshake and sings our
sacred, solemn songs. Yet when I see their horseshoe-
shaped brands, I sometimes have to fight back a pang of
guilt when I look at my own bare skin.

Branding, the literal burning into the flesh of the fraternity's symbol—the last letter of the Greek alphabet—
is the final step of the initiation. For me, the brands do not
evoke images of conquered black men in chains as chattel.
On the contrary, I see the marks as a sign of pride and
brotherhood. I believe they reflect a kind of spirituality
and beauty through sacrifice that is at the core of the
African aesthetic. When I pledged, branding was optional,
but few refused it.

Hours before the start of my initiation ceremony, however, I told my soon-to-be fraternity brothers that I did not want a brand—at least, not on my chest. Putting the brand near the heart was the custom of my local chapter. That was not how I had imagined it.

I had grown up in a working-class neighborhood in Louisville, Kentucky, where the thought of someone branding his skin was as foreign as worshiping cows. While a high school freshman, however, I began to reconsider. One afternoon some Omega brothers visited my school, which was predominately black and best known for winning basketball games. These guys wore purple jackets with gold-colored letters so oddly formed I had first mistaken them for letters of the Russian alphabet.

For me, these men were clearly part of something special, something not just anybody could join. Their fraternity, they explained, was something that required hard work, struggle, and perseverance.

It was founded at Howard University shortly after the turn of the century, grounded in principles that emphasized leadership, academic excellence, and a commitment to service in the black community. Of course they had a good time, throwing dances and being men about campus, but they didn't brag about beer parties and panty raids. They talked, instead, about scholarship drives, tutoring for the college-bound, and setting up networks with other people of action, whether they were in fraternities or not.

They told me Jesse Jackson was an Omega man. So were Bill Cosby and Charles Drew, the doctor who developed the technique for storing plasma in blood banks.

Omegas were as serious as the times. I wanted to be part of what they represented. I also began to convince myself that I wanted to wear their symbol—three inches high and two inches wide—like they did. For life.

But two years later, on the morning of my initiation, I was confronted by an overweight guy in a tight T-shirt. He was holding a makeshift branding iron fashioned from a wire clothes hanger and reddened on an electric hot plate.

"So, are you going to get one on your chest or not?" he asked, thinking that I might have changed my mind. His voice was weary from screaming at me the night before during a final pledge test called hell night.

"I want it on my arm," I said pointing to my baby-smooth biceps.

"Tradition says you get it on the chest first and then anywhere else you want it after that."

"Naw," I said, "my arm."

"If you don't get a brand on the chest, you don't get one at all," he replied before preparing the iron for another branding.

I was disappointed, but the idea of marking my chest somehow didn't appeal to me. Marking an arm, especially with a wound across the muscled bulge of my biceps, seemed so warriorlike. So manly.

Besides, Omegas had a reputation for hard, sometimes even brutal, pledging. We called ourselves the "sons of blood and thunder" and meant it. A visible brand could have been my medal of valor and honor rolled into one.

Machismo personified. A brand made a tattoo look like

a bad ink stain, I thought. But for me, it had to be on my arm; nowhere else would do.

I had nothing to be ashamed of, I reasoned. I had passed all the tests, and had won the respect of my new brothers while gaining a higher respect for myself. I was an Omega man, simply one without its insignia on my skin.

On that morning, something prevented me from caving in to what seemed like subtle peer pressure to burn my skin in a place I was not prepared to. Once I refused, however, the fraternity brothers seemed sincerely undisturbed by my decision; I was not browbeaten by the branded because I had decided to be brandless. One even suggested that I might change my mind and get it later.

"I might," I said with equal sincerity.

Perhaps my strength was drawn from the sum of the many lessons I had already learned from pledging. Through the more than two months of hardships and joys that led to my admission into the tribe, I had discovered that an essential element of being a man was the possession of an unblinking vision that can see beyond the immediate.

That when there is a common interest among men who have gained one another's respect and trust, compassion and understanding often follow.

My composure and clarity did not flee as I watched another brother receive his brand to cheers and congratulatory backslaps. One of the students I had pledged with got a brand on his chest, left buttock, right thigh, and left arm. He said no matter where or how he stood, he always wanted an omega to face the sun. I saluted him for his personal choice. Yet I clung to my resolve and finished the ceremony, with its candlelight and whispered rituals, brandless but more of an Omega than even I, at the time, realized.

MICHEL MARRIOTT

A MATTER OF TRUST

⚜

MY SON is trustworthy. I knew that. Or thought I knew it, and that I could trust him. Still, I'm his mother and I couldn't help but wait up for him until he returned home when he went out. You know the trouble teenagers can get into. You know the trouble that can get into them. So, on this one night, like scores of others nights before, I was waiting up for him. I started out by reading, then switched on the television for the eleven o'clock news, then tuned to some talk radio show to stay awake. One o'clock. No son. No call. His curfew, and I am a little disturbed that he isn't striding through the door or at least phoning to say he'd be a few minutes late. One fifteen. Still no son. Still no call. I feel the blood rushing to the surface of my skin. I'm angry now. Do I really have to italicize the fact that I want him ON TIME, and failing that, for unforeseen circumstances, to CALL. I turn off the murmuring radio and pace in the hallway. On a yellow legal pad I remember him doodling around the numbers of a couple of boys with whom he is supposed to be. Should I possibly embarrass myself by calling during my avalanching anger? Or worse, panic their parents with a call in the middle of the night. What was the name of the restaurant? Ah yes, the Hickory Stick, a rib joint. I call information and then the restaurant. Ringing, ringing, and I am muttering under my breath. No answer. I slam down the phone in frustration, anger, and frankly a little bit of panic, when I hear a voice call out, "Is that you, Mom?" Groggy, husky with sleep and the inconsistent timbre of adolescence finding its range, the voice wafts from the first-floor landing. Turns out the gathering of his was not all that, after all, and my son came home early when I was in the basement washing clothes. He had called out, thought he heard my response, then immediately gone to bed. I was relieved and ashamed—ashamed not of being worried, but of being angry. Teenager or not, I should know my son enough to know that he wouldn't be so irresponsible as to not check in. I hugged him, but tried not to squeeze too tight. My son is trustworthy. I knew that. I know it still.

AS TOLD TO ERIC V. COPAGE

NOTHING TO FEAR

❦

ON THE SPEECH circuit, I tell a story that goes to the heart of America's longing. The ABC correspondent Sam Donaldson was interviewing a young African-American soldier in a tank platoon on the eve of the battle in Desert Storm. Donaldson asked, "How do you think the battle will go? Are you afraid?"

"We'll do okay. We're well trained. And I'm not afraid," the GI answered, gesturing toward his buddies around him. "I'm not afraid because I'm with my family."

The other soldiers shouted, "Tell him again. He didn't hear you."

The soldier repeated, "This is my family and we'll take care of each other."

That story never fails to touch me or the audience. It is a metaphor for what we have to do as a nation. We have to start thinking of America as a family. We have to stop screeching at each other, stop hurting each other, and instead start caring for, sacrificing for, and sharing with each other. We have to stop constantly criticizing, which is the way of the malcontent, and instead get back to the can-do attitude that made America. We have to keep trying, and risk failing, in order to solve this country's problems. We cannot move forward if cynics and critics swoop down and pick apart anything that goes wrong to a point where we lose sight of what is right, decent, and uniquely good about America.

COLIN POWELL,
from *My American Journey*

WEIGHT IN GOLD

❧

"Like Billy Eckstine and Frank Sinatra's sons, I wish I was rich enough to be kidnapped," said Simple, "because if I was, I would have done spent all my money before the kidnapping happened. I would never let them hold me for ransom, because the ransom money would be gone. I would just say, 'Boys, you have come too late. My pockets and my bank account is both now turned inside out. I have run through my million. Better to have had and spent than never to have had at all.'"

"My dear fellow," I countered, "if you ever possessed a great deal of money, say a million or so, you would find it next to impossible to spend it all. Besides, if you were sensible, you would invest the principal and live on the interest, like most rich people do."

"I would not be sensible," said Simple. "If I had money, I would go stark-raving mad and spend it! I could not stand being rich. There is so much I have wanted in past days, and so much I still want now—I would just spend it all, yes. And what I did not spend, I would give away to peoples I love. I would give Joyce, my wife, One Hundred Thousand Dollars. I would look up Zarita, that old gal of mine, and for old times' sake, I would give her Fifty Thousand Dollars. To you, Boyd, my old beer buddy, I would give Twenty-five Thousand, and to my Cousin Mini, Ten, so she would not have to borrow from me any-more. Also, I would present Mini with a brand-new wig, since she lost hers in the riots. And for every neighbor kid I know, I would buy a bicycle, because I think every boy—and girl, too, if they wants—should have a bicycle while young."

"In this New York traffic, as heavy as it is, you would give kids bicycles?"

"They can always ride in Central Park," said Simple. "When I were a kid, I always wanted a bicycle, and nobody ever bought me one. To tell you the truth, if I was rich I would buy myself a bicycle right now. Then next month I would buy me a motorcycle. I always wanted one of them to make noise on. Then after riding around on my motorcycle for a couple of weeks, I would buy me a small car, just big enough for Joyce and me. After which I would buy a big car, then a Town and Country, then a sta-tion wagon. After that I would get a foreign sports car. I would do this gradual, not letting the world know all at once that I am rich. Also, I would not like to be kidnapped until all the money was spent. I would like to have my fun first, then be kidnapped with my name in the papers,

'Jesse B. Semple Nabbed by Mob. *Held for Ransom, Harlem Shaken by the News.*'"

"You would be missed in the bar," I said.

"If I was rich, I would own this bar," said Simple. "I would buy up all the bars in Harlem and keep the present white proprietors employed as managers. I would not draw any color line. Of course, if the white men quit and did not want to work under me, black, I would go to HARYOU and ask them to send me some bright young colored managers."

"HARYOU?" I said. "HARYOU hardly supplies bartenders, does it?"

"I would not request bartenders," said Simple. "I would be employing colored *managers*. They tell me HARYOU is set up to give young Negroes a chance."

"Why, tell me, please, if you had money," I asked, "would you buy only bars? Why not restaurants, grocery stores, clothing shops, wiggeries?"

"Because bars has the quickest turnover," said Simple. "Besides, if I owned all the Harlem bars, I would have credit in each and every one of them. I would never have to ask anybody to buy me a beer. In fact, I would treat *you* every time we met. Oh, if I was rich, daddy-o, I would be a generous son of a gun, 'specially with everybody I like. I not only like you, Boyd, but I admire you. You are colleged. You know, if I had money, I would send every young man and young woman in Harlem to college, that wanted to go. I would set up one of these offices that gives out money for education."

"You mean a Foundation for Fellowships," I said.

"And girlships, too," declared Simple. "Women and mens from Harlem would all be colleged by the time 1970 came. It do not take but four years to get colleged, do it?"

"That's right," I said. "Depending on your application."

"I would tell all the boys and girls in Harlem to make their applications now," said Simple, "and I would see that they got through. White folks downtown would have no excuse anymore to say we was not educated uptown, because I would pay for it."

"In other words, you would be Harlem's Ford Foundation," I said, "on a really big scale."

"Yes," said Simple, "because on my scales, every kid in Harlem is worth his weight in gold."

LANGSTON HUGHES,
from *The Return of Simple*

RECIPE FOR FAMILY

❧❧❧

T HE WORD *family* has a thousand definitions. You can talk about the biological ties of the nearest of kin—father, mother, brother, sister. You can talk about the next circle of cousins, aunts, uncles, and grandparents where the presence of dimples, a high forehead, or a crooked smile indicate an intimate stew of shared DNA that reaches back before recorded history. There is also family at a more abstract level—a classroom, a sports team, a club, a political party, citizens of a given city, state, or country. Sometimes we feel we have more in common with our adopted families of choice than we do with our biological families. If we are lucky, however, we have a number of different families, comprised of relatives, friends, civic associations, and so forth, and each of these different families contributes to our well-being in a unique way. But all families need to be cultivated, nurtured, and nourished. They need time to be reunited and renewed. In this increasingly hectic world in which we live, however, that can be difficult. A way to make it manageable is to take five minutes every day to reconnect with a given friend, loved one, or family member, and thereby renew that relationship and create a stronger unit.

Take five minutes to encourage a family member to tell you something good that is happening in his or her life.

Take five minutes to share one of your interests.

Take five minutes and offer to be an ear for anything that might be troubling a family member.

Take five minutes to solicit their advice on one of your problems.

Take five minutes and encourage a family member to tell you about a dream.

Take five minutes to share one of your dreams.

Take five minutes and congratulate a family member on a success.

Take five minutes to console one after a defeat.

Take five minutes to tell a family member something for which you respect that person.

Take five minutes to look into your soul and forgive them for real or imagined wrongs they have done you.

ERIC V. COPAGE

Creativity

BLACK AMERICAN LITERATURE: AN INTRODUCTION

A FEW YEARS AGO, *Voyager 2* crossed our galaxy heading toward the Dog Star. We don't know a lot about the light that earth sees, but we know the brightest star in the galaxy is beyond the influence of the yellow sun. Galileo would be proud. I'm a Trekkie. I like the concepts of both space and the future. I'm not big on the idea of aliens who always seem to want to destroy earth and earthlings. It's almost laughable that the most destructive force in the known universe, humankind, always fears something is out there trying to get us. Freud said something about projection . . . and though I would hardly consider myself a Freudian, I think he had a point.

It's not really a question of whether or not E.T. is Black; his story is the story of sojourning. It doesn't even matter whether he came to earth to explore or was brought to earth for less honorable pursuits. He found himself left behind with neither kith nor kin to turn to. He depended, in the words of Tennessee Williams, "upon the kindness of strangers." E.T. didn't sing, but if he had he would have raised his voice to say, "Sometimes I feel like a motherless child . . . a long way from home." E.T., had he taken the time to assess his situation, may have lifted his voice to the sky to say, "I'm going to fly away . . . one of these days . . . I'm going to fly away." When the men with the keys captured him, taking him to the laboratory to dissect him, to open him up in order to find what he was made of, he might have hummed, "You got to walk this lonesome valley . . . you got to walk it by yourself." But E.T., like Dorothy, had friends who came to his rescue. Dorothy returned to Kansas more sensitive, more aware of her world. E.T. returned to space having, I'm sure, a mixed view of earth. Black Americans settled here, making a stand for humanity.

It is an honorable position . . . to be a Black American. Our spirituals teach, "I've been 'buked and I've been scorned . . . I've been talked about sure as I'm born." We maintained an oral tradition and created a written one. Phillis Wheatley, a slave girl, wrote poetry while others sang our songs. We did both because both are necessary. Hammer, while different form, is not in contrast to Frederick Douglass. Two Live Crew is in a direct line with Big Mama Thornton and all the other blues singers who sang what is called the "race music." (The "good" people would not allow it in their churches or homes.) But we have survived and thrived because of our ability to find the sacred in the secular. "Oh, pray my wings gonna fit me well," says the song, but whether they fit ill or well, we wear what we have with style.

Style has a profound meaning to Black Americans. If we can't drive, we will invent walks and the world will envy the dexterity of our feet. If we can't have ham, we will boil chitterlings; if we are given rotten peaches, we will make cobblers; if given scraps, we will make quilts; take away our drums, and we will clap our hands. We prove the human spirit will prevail. We will take what we have to make what we need. We need confidence in our knowledge of who we are.

America is no longer a nation of rural people. We no longer go to visit Grandmother and Grandfather on the farm in the summer. This is no longer a nation where the daily work is done by the body; the daily work is now performed by the mind. The distance between families is no longer a walk or even a short drive. Families, for that matter, are no longer clear. Biology no longer defines whom we love or relate to. We are now able to make emotional choices. There is so much to be done to prepare earth for the next century. Humans, who are so fearful of change, are in such a radical transition. The literature of Black Americans can lead the way. As we were once thrown into a physical unknown where our belief in the wonder of life helped forge a new nation, we can help lead earth into an emotional unknown and seek acceptance for those who are unique. Our literature shows that humans can withstand the unacceptable and yet still find a way to forgive. Our stories, which once were passed sitting on porches after dinner, spitting tobacco juice at fireflies, as Alex Haley's grandmother did, are now passed through the poems, speeches, stories we have written and recorded.

While a bowl of navy beans is one of my favorite meals (with a bit of cole slaw and corn muffins on the side), I still enjoy a smorgasbord. Sometimes a bit of everything creates an appetite while satisfying a hunger. For all the trouble we now understand the voyage of Columbus to have caused, it must have been exciting to live in an age when we finally began to break into a concept of the whole earth. For sure, we have not done a great job, but we have done a better job than if we had stayed home. This century is rolling on to a close. There is both outer space and inner space to be explored. The literature of Black Americans is, in the words of Stevie Wonder, "a ribbon in the sky." We learn about and love the past because it gives us the courage to explore and take care of the future. *Voyager 2* will not come back . . . it has gone too far away. We will not return, we can only visit. But isn't it a comforting thought to realize that the true pioneer of earth is our people? Isn't it the ultimate challenge to accept responsibility not only for ourselves but for our planet? One day, some identifiable life form will come to earth and ask, "Who are these people . . . these Black Americans?" And we will proudly present our book containing our songs, plays, speeches, and poetry. We will proudly say, "We are the people who believe in the possibilities."

NIKKI GIOVANNI,
from *Racism 101*

TRANSFORMATION

W HEN I WAS BORN in 1903, my father was a farmer in Louisiana. But when bad weather caused him to lose all of his crops, the family moved to Austin, Texas, which was a land of opportunity at that time. In Austin my father worked for a man who owned a drugstore and catered wedding receptions and anniversary parties. My mother was a seamstress. She could design clothes from a picture or a thought. There were six of us children, and we were a family of survivors.

Sometimes my mother would close up the house, and somebody would come and get us in a truck or a wagon, and we'd go to a town miles away to pick cotton. We would stay there in a cabin for about a month or as long as it took us to pick the field. We learned to make what we needed from what we had. For example, the stores bought flour, sugar, bran, and chicken feed in thirty-six-inch-square muslin bags. We'd buy those bags for twenty-five cents, or the store owner would give them to us, and we'd use them to make clothes, sheets, towels, and curtains. First, we'd soak the bags in cold water to take the writing off, then we would wash them in ash water that we made by putting ashes in water. After the ashes settled, the water would be like lye, and it would bleach the muslin white and pretty. One bag would make a pillow case, a skirt, a shirt, or a blouse. We sewed four together to make a sheet, and we briar-stitched the seams and embroidered the hems to make it pretty. A bag was cut in half to make a towel or a curtain, and in four pieces to make washcloths. We always added embroidery, briar-stitching, and crochet for decoration. The things we made were beautiful.

ADA DEBLANC SIMOND,
from *Talk That Talk*, edited by
Marion E. Barnes and Linda Goss

A MOTHER'S SMILE

I WAS SPENDING more and more time on the road, sometimes going a couple months without seeing Mom. I was no mama's boy and glad to be out on my own, but the truth is, I missed her. Mom never came right out and said she didn't want me singing rock 'n' roll and R&B, but I knew full well that she would have preferred that I keep my singing in the church. I also knew there were elements of show business life it was better she didn't know about. She would not have approved of or understood some of the circles I now traveled in or some of the things I was doing. Although it was hard to admit, the fact that she still hadn't seen me perform weighed heavily on my heart.

One night that I won't forget, we played a very small club in downtown Baltimore, across the street from a bus station. The show had begun, we were singing, and the houselights were down. From the stage, it's impossible to make out anything beyond the first couple of rows of tables and chairs, but your eye is automatically drawn to movement in the crowd. I sensed her presence before I even saw her.

Looking toward the back of the club, I spotted two figures who I instinctively knew were Mom and Aunt Persephone. I knew Mom by the way she was moving across the room. I'd seen it a million times in church: Very politely, very humbly, she would bend slightly at the waist and raise her index finger as if to say, "Excuse me, please" as she made her way across a crowded pew.

When I realized it was Mom, I was thrilled and nervous as hell! Let me tell you, that night I sang my butt off. I had something to prove and a mission to accomplish: I was going to make her like what I was singing. When the show was over, I rushed down to her table, where she was seated with my aunt. "Wow, Mom," I said breathlessly, "what are you doing here?"

And my mother, cool as can be, replied, "Oh, we just decided to come down and see you and see how you were doing."

"This calls for champagne, then," I said, then without thinking, added, "Mom, would you like some champagne?"

"No, no I don't drink." I knew that! Where was my head?

"Well, Mom, we'll get you some ginger ale in a champagne glass. That way you can look like you're sipping champagne," I suggested, and she smiled. We toasted, and suddenly it was like everything was okay. I was a grown man out on my own, but knowing that my mother approved of me and what I was doing was the most comforting feeling in the world.

Later, Mom told me she thought to herself as she watched me that night, Look what I have, look what God gave me. I could tell that she approved of what I was doing and believed in me, although she didn't say that to me back then. (Actually she told me this while I was writing this book.) But from the look on her face, I knew. Now there was nothing I couldn't do.

TEDDY PENDERGRASS,
from *Truly Blessed*

THE CHOICE

❦

HE WHO CALLED himself master stood before the man who was enslaved. The man was bent, the result of the latest lashings he had endured, but not broken. The man had tried to escape again. His feet were as raw as his back from having traveled over rocks and fallen branches on his way to freedom. The man's feet were still numb from having splashed through swamps, rivers, and marshes so that the dogs would not pick up his scent. But the dogs and he who called himself master had caught up with the man, and brought him back to the plantation. And he had been whipped in front of the other enslaved Africans as an example to all.

But the man remained unbroken, and he who called himself master could see the defiance in the man's eyes. The other enslaved Africans bore witness, too, as did a smattering of the other planters, their wives, and children who were visiting he who called himself master. He had to reassert his power, but he had to do it in a way which didn't look gratuitous. Which didn't look wanton. The man had already endured forty lashes and remained conscious and upright. No man had ever done that before. Suddenly he lit upon an idea.

"You want your freedom," he said, drawing out his words with great ceremony, playing to the crowd. "Well, then, I'll give you a chance to grab it." A cruel smile came across his face. "But if you lose I will give you another forty lashes. And you have to promise never to try to escape again."

The man who was not broken looked around slowly at the astonished faces, black and white, that gazed at him. The man silently wondered: What is this chance for freedom? This supposed master is a cruel creature, the man thought. Whatever test or gamble he has devised will only provide an excuse for him to beat me further.

Still, the man felt he couldn't let this opportunity go by, for it was an opportunity no matter the cruel intent. The man felt the blood oozing down his back and breezes coursing over the open wounds.

"I'll take your wager," the man said, with all the strength he could muster.

The smile on the so-called master's face broadened, narrowing his eyes into slits. He knew that the man had no real choice but to walk into the trap. He took two small pieces of paper, scribbled something on each, folded them so that they could not be deciphered without opening them, and walked toward the man.

"I have in my hand two squares of paper," he said tauntingly. "One says freedom, the other says slavery. Pick the one that says *freedom*, and I will give you your papers and you may leave. Choose the one that says *slavery* and you must vow to stay here for the rest of your days without hope of freedom. And you must submit to another forty lashes."

The so-called master put his hand behind his back and with great ceremony passed the papers back and forth from one hand to the other. He then stuck out both arms. "Choose," he demanded.

The man looked at the identical pieces of paper, held between the thumb and forefinger of the so-called master's hands. The papers flinched slightly in the breeze, but the so-called master's hands were steady. Cruel as he was, he was no fool. He had no intention of letting loose his chattel, the creature he had paid so dearly for. His one goal was to set an example. He didn't write *slavery* on one piece of paper and *freedom* on the other. He wrote *slavery* on both. No matter which paper the man chose he was doomed to continued enslavement.

But the African was no fool, either. He knew that he who called himself master really believed that he was a master, and would not relinquish the title easily. The man had figured out that the creature who called himself master had devised some trick. Just what kind of trick and how to thwart it were what remained to be figured out.

The June sun had burned the morning mist away, and the man was beginning to feel the sun's rays stinging into his open wounds. He longed for balm, some unguent to soothe the wounds. He longed also for a solution to the problem that fevered his brain.

Suddenly, something impacted his entire body. The man felt a shudder, as if he had been struck by a bolt of lightning. He felt a reverberation in his soul, and knew it was the spirit of God. The man reached for one of the folded pieces of paper, grabbed it, and quickly swallowed it.

"What do you have in your hand?" the African asked. "For if you have freedom I must have slavery and will submit to your forty lashes and stand by my vow never to try to escape again. But if you have slavery, then I must have chosen freedom. And by your word, I am free to go."

He who called himself master was stunned. He had never imagined this would be how his cruel game would end. There was a long silence, and the crowd, black and white, held its breath, waiting to see what would happen next. He who called himself master slowly crumpled the remaining paper in his hand and began putting it in his pocket.

"Let's see the paper," a fellow plantation owner called out. And the demand was taken up by the other white plantation owners, and their wives and daughters and sons, and even a few of the enslaved Africans. "Let's see the paper," the plantation owner repeated. "Let's see if your slave has won his freedom."

The so-called master slowly passed the still-crumpled paper to the other plantation owner, who opened it and then looked at the African.

"Looks like today is your lucky day," the plantation

owner said. "According to the rules of this game, looks like you just plucked your way to freedom."

And so the African said his good-byes to the enslaved Africans. There were hugs. There were kisses. There were tears. He was given a sack with biscuits and dried meat. And then he walked down the plantation's long pathway and along the road toward freedom, until the plantation house was obscured by trees. Once the African got settled up North, he established himself as an ironsmith, then became a conductor on the underground railroad, allowing his house to be used as a way station for other Africans who were finding their way to freedom.

AS TOLD TO ERIC V. COPAGE

THE ECHO THAT NEVER FADES

I PICKED UP a pencil and held it over a sheet of white paper, but my feelings stood in the way of my words. Well, I would wait, day and night, until I knew what to say. Humbly now, with no vaulting dream of achieving a vast unity, I wanted to try to build a bridge of words between me and that world outside, that world which was so distant and elusive that it seemed unreal.

I would hurl words into this darkness and wait for an echo, and if an echo sounded, no matter how faintly, I would send other words to tell, to march, to fight, to create a sense of the hunger for life that gnaws in us all, to keep alive in our hearts a sense of the inexpressibly human.

RICHARD WRIGHT,
from *Black Boy*

THE MOUTH OF THE CAVE

I HAVE DISCOVERED PAINT. Mixing the water with the powder makes color bright and primary. I imagine that I have returned to the cave of my childhood dreams, to the paintings on the wall. The art teacher, Mr. Harold, watches me stirring. He tells me he has been watching me since class began, that he enjoys the sight of a student falling in love with color again and again. He brings me a stack of paper. I wait always before I begin painting. He says I take too long, that such intense concentration may block the creativity. I want him to leave me alone. I am silent. He understands. He will come back later. I am trying to remember the pictures in the cave, the animals. If I can paint them all I am sure I can discover again the secret of living, what it was I left in the cave. I start with the color black. In a book on the history of pigment I come across a new phrase, *bone black*. Bone black is a black carbonaceous substance obtained by calcifying bones in closed vessels. Burning bones, that's what it makes me think about—flesh on fire, turning black, turning into ash.

Mr. Harold laughs when I tell him that all my life I have heard my mother say black is a woman's color—a color denied me because I am a child. He wears black pants and black shirts with funny ties. He can look this way because he is the art teacher, because he is an artist. In this integrated high school he is one of the few white teachers who does not keep black kids at arm's length, who is not afraid. He cares. He is the only one who seems to understand that the whites and their hatreds are the problem and not us. He does not deny us. He does not deny me the color black. He urges me to stay with it but to add color, to do more with it.

I begin with the mouth of the cave, add red to the black. The red is the heart of the seekers, the animals and human beings who come. The next picture is one of the fire. Up close, with outstretched hands feeling the warmth, I remember that the fire is not just the color red, that it is blue and yellow and green. These are the colors of the lost spirits. Mixed together they bring new life to color. At the bottom of the fire is the color black. This is the ash that the fire becomes. This is the remains of all the animals who have given their life in sacrifice to keep the spirit moving, burning bright. I want to make the color gray, to paint a world covered in mist, but this painting must wait, for it is what I see when I leave the cave. The animals must be painted. I try and try but cannot get them right. Mr. Harold looks at me from his desk and says "no" as he sees me about to rip the paper, to throw it away. He shakes his head "no." He has told me many times to keep at it, to look at it, to rethink what it is I am trying to do. Without remembering all the animals I leave watercolor behind; I am on to acrylic, to painting on canvas.

The color black is sometimes harsh. I abandon it now and then for the colors red, yellow, and brown. The picture I am painting is of the wilderness my spirit roams in. I tell him that I left the cave and went into the wilderness. He tells me to let the colors show what the wilderness is like. All around are fading colors that contain bits of pieces of their earlier brightness. I call this painting *Autumn in the Wilderness*.

BELL HOOKS,
from *Bone Black*

DEFYING GRAVITY

❧

MARTHA GRAHAM'S COMPANY came to Binghamton that year.

I knew who Martha Raye was. I knew who Martha Washington was. But who in the hell was this Martha Graham? I didn't go to the performance. The following day, I saw photographs of the dancers in the school newspaper. While akin to that of *West Side Story,* with its faux Puerto Ricans strutting down the street, snapping their fingers, slicing the air with their left hands while striking the ground with their feet, this dance ran much deeper. Its implications were ancient. As ancient as the rites and pageantry inscribed on Hellenic urns. These dancers, these men and women, were not mortal at all, but the creatures of legend and myth. Their heat and exuberance, their pasts and futures, were caught in the images reproduced on the newsprint. Even my untrained eyes could recognize this.

Soon, time that I was supposed to spend researching and writing papers I spent poring through books on the arts—painting, architecture, theater, music. And the dance books needed no captions, no explanation. I lived the images that I found in them, commanded them to move in my body, in my imagination. When I saw a dancer's arm reaching toward heaven, I reached, too. When I witnessed the impossible pitch of a Gambian shaman dancer, I experienced the giddy defiance of gravity.

I saw a film of Balanchine's *Tchaikovsky Pas de Deux:* Suzanne Farrell ran forward without warning, threw herself upward, backward into the air, trusting her male partner to catch her. They stopped. The music stopped. This perfect emphasis suggested the possibility of a body suspended in air for all of time. I was suspended. I wanted this possibility. I wanted to pitch and turn, lunge and strike down the halls of the Fine Arts Building or across the campus. In an empty dance studio, enjoying the curious comfort of watching the way my body, reflected in the mirror, affected space as I changed my position. I would sing quietly to myself as I wafted and soared about, my imagination ignoring all thresholds.

In these moments, I was creator, performer, and audience. I experienced the deep truth of movement. How to share this with others was something I would struggle with for years.

When members of the Utah Repertory Dance Theater came to Binghamton to perform and give master classes, Mrs. Grandy divided us into two groups—those who were allowed to take classes and those who could only watch. I could only watch.

Tim Wengerd stepped out on the floor. He was a strongly built man with an ample square face and wide-set, almost Asian eyes. He inhaled sharply, then attacked the space before him. With both arms outstretched, his left foot took his weight while his right leg came up sharply as if to kick. Then, with an unexpected change of intent, it bent at the knee and ankle, swiveled viciously in the hip socket as his foot—with the precision of a bullet piercing a target—found the floor and invited his massive body earthward. He had sailed serenely in an arc of such sureness and purity. An imitation of his movement I would never achieve, but its essential nature was mine from that moment on.

BILL T. JONES,
from *Last Night on Earth*

THE BEST BIRTHDAY PRESENT EVER

M Y DAUGHTER gave me a ceramic picture frame one day. It wasn't brightly colored or shiny or glazed. It wasn't a smooth oval nor a perfect square.

She had made it as a present for my birthday at her school's after care class. When I walked in to pick up my daugther, the instructor pulled me aside to warn me that my seven year old was in tears.

"She was so enthusiastic that she just went on and did things without waiting for my help," the instructor said contritely. "She was just so eager and impatient to make you the perfect gift that she touched the clay before it was dry and put the paint on too soon. It has the imprints from her fingers and the colors ran together. I'm afraid that it is a bit of a mess, and she is quite sad about it."

I couldn't help but wonder if there was anything else inside that sadness. My husband had recently died of cancer. It wasn't a pretty sight. And as much as both he—while he had the strength—and I tried to brace her for the eventuality of his death, as much as she must have seen him virtually wither away before her eyes in a matter of weeks, his passing hit her like a jolt from the third rail. My family tried to coax her from the shell she formed around herself in the aftermath of his death. They offered her hugs and kisses and love. And so did I, but that wasn't enough. And so there were school counselors and counselors I employed from the outside. My daughter was still sealed inside herself.

And then, just last month, she mentioned my birthday—how she wanted to do something special for it. I was thrilled because it was the first sign that she was getting back to her old self. Her ebullient and creative and mischievous self. She had refused to tell me what she was going to do for my birthday. "It's a secret," she said with the exaggerated whisper of a stage actress. Then she tiptoed away.

The after care instructor led me to a corner of the cafeteria, where my daughter had isolated herself in a corner, her head in her arms on the lunch table. She was still. I approached her with my best smile and let her know Mommy was there with my cheeriest hello.

She picked her head up and turned it slowly in my direction. Her mahogany-colored cheeks were streaked from the salt of dried tears. When she saw me, the tears started flowing again.

Once we arrived home, she ran up to her room, holding the crumpled brown paper bag in which she had hidden the picture frame that had so disappointed her. I left her alone; I knew that she needed some space. But with dinner about to be served, I knocked on her door.

"Sweetie," I said, and told her dinner was ready. She told me she didn't want to eat. I entered the room. She was looking glumly out the window.

"Mommy," she cried, "why can't I do anything right? I wanted this to be the best present for you ever. I've made it the worst birthday ever, I mess up everything."

I gently held her face in both my hands and smiled.

"Honey," I said, "this *is* the best birthday I have ever had. And you've helped make it so, with your love and your kindness and your good thoughts. But you know what you could do to make it even better? Let me see the frame, sweetheart. Let me see what you've done and you will make this the best birthday I have had in my entire life."

She walked to the trash basket. It was still in the bag she had hidden it in.

Reluctantly, she took it out and held it before me.

No, it wasn't perfect. But it was perfection. Her hand-prints personalized it in the most marvelous way. And yes, it was lopsided, but this gave it life and energy. It wasn't just a symmetrical desktop ornament. The black was uneven and punctuated with irregular splashes of gold and silver. Was it something that would have sold for a fortune at Christie's? I don't know. All I can say is that it brought tears to my eyes.

I tried to hide my tears. Lord knows how my daughter would have interpreted them, given the mood she was in. But I took the frame in my hand.

"Look at this," I said to her. "You've taken lifeless clay and given it life. Made it breathe. Made it sparkle. I'm going to take this to work, where I will keep this on my desk always, so that I can always be reminded of you and how you made this the most wonderful birthday in my entire life."

And I was true to my word. The frame my daughter made for me fourteen years ago still sits on the desk in my office today. And over the years it has protected many a photograph of her—from when she was seven and coming to terms with the death of her father, as a young teenager going through the first pangs of adulthood, to her graduation from college. The graduation photograph is of her and me horsing around on the campus lawn right after the ceremony. That frame has encircled our lives with goodness and prayer. And the frame so imperfectly crafted was created by an angel, and has formed a protective and perfect halo around our lives.

AS TOLD TO ERIC V. COPAGE

RECIPE FOR CREATIVITY

꧁⚜꧂

WHEN PEOPLE THINK of creativity, they
most often think about vast and intimidating
artistic projects—the musical innovations of
Miles Davis and Beethoven, the soulful paintings of
Romare Bearden and Michelangelo. In fact, creativity is
just being playful with the world; you can even be creative
when, say, discussing the relative merits of sports figures.
Is Muhammad Ali the greatest boxer of all time? Well,
how do you define greatness? Do you mean pound for
pound or do you mean in the heavyweight category? Do
you mean knock outs or do you mean wins? What would
happen if in your mind's eye, you put Ali against Rocky
Marciano. Against Mike Tyson? What would be the likely
outcome? Why? In other words, creativity is a matter of
taking something and seeing it in a different context. It is
a process of imagination that works in spurts of inspira-

tion prodded by the perspiration of problem-solving techniques that are learnable. This kind of thinking works in the most mundane situations—getting an oversize bed up the stairs and into a bedroom, getting a new job, trying to get your child to behave—and in the same way as it does in solving scientific quandaries. Here are just a few tips for living a more creative life.

1. Ask questions of yourself. Seek suggestions from others.

2. Never be afraid to be too obvious. You walk outside and the doors shut on you. Is it really locked? Try the door knob. Did you really forget your keys inside? Check your pockets.

3. Define what the problem is about. Is the door locked or just jammed? Is the problem about opening the door or getting inside your apartment? If it is about getting inside, any entrance should do. Try a ground floor window.

4. Be alert to what is going on in the world near and far. You might have seen something on a comedy or crime show that might give you ideas about how to get into your house.

5. Be metaphorical and imaginative in thinking about the problem. Is getting into your apartment like getting into Fort Knox? Like getting into a locked car? Like getting a secret out of a friend? Let your imagination wander and it might help you think about the problem in a different way and thereby present a viable solution.

6. Try reversing the situation. For instance, if a door doesn't open when you push it, see what happens if you pull it.

7. Think about modifying a situation in ways other than reversing it. For instance, in trying to open that shut door, what happens if you try to lift it, or lower it while pushing or pulling it?

8. Think about the ramifications of a given action. For instance, if you push or pull the door too hard, is it possible that you will break the door knob? And if you do, is it likely that you will gain entry into the house that way, or is it likely to make opening the door more difficult?

9. Reverse one element in a situation. You tried turning the door knob clockwise to open it; try counter clockwise.

10. Have you ever been in a similar situation? If so, figure out how you solved the problem then and try it again in the present situation. Perhaps you once got locked out and used a knife or something slender to slip between the door and the door frame. Might that work in this instance?

11. What are the constituent parts of a situation? You are locked out of your apartment. The important thing is getting in, not opening the door per se. You have an oak door, glass, locks on the windows, the door knob, the door frame. . . .

As I said, these are only a few suggestions. Entire books have been written on the subject. But this should get you started in bringing creativity to life's problems. And as for writing, painting, dancing, singing, composing, sculpting—these are some of the things that make life wonderful. It's never too late to start. Try them.

ERIC V. COPAGE

Tenacity

HUNGRY FOR AIRTIME

❧

So, to become a radio disc jockey, I practiced and practiced to improve. I worked on my delivery and technical skills every day for weeks and weeks. And finally I went to the radio station that I had targeted in Miami, and I asked for the program director, Mr. Milton "Butterball" Smith.

I had to go down there during my lunch break from my mowing job, and old Butterball looked at my overalls and my straw hat and said, "Do you have any radio experience?"

"No, sir, I don't," I said.

"Do you have any journalism background?"

"No, sir, I don't," I replied. "But I can never get it if you don't give me the opportunity. I've been practicing a lot, sir."

"I'm sorry," he said. "We don't have a job for you."

I thanked him and left. But I was not defeated. You see,

he did not know my purpose for being there. I wanted to become a disc jockey, yes, but my deeper purpose was to buy my mother a house. I had a big dream for a grass cutter. But I also had a big hunger.

My favorite program on television back then was *The Millionaire*. It was the show in which the central character, Michael Anthony, would search someone out and present that person each week with a check for one million dollars.

That was my fantasy, to get a million dollars so I could buy my mother one of those big homes on Miami Beach. And so, after Butterball rolled right over me, I went back and talked with [my teacher] Mr. Washington. He told me not to take it personally. He said some people are so negative they have to say no seven times before they say yes.

He told me to go back to Butterball. So the next day I went back to the station and said, "Hello, Mr. Butterball, how are you doing? My name is Les Brown."

"I know your name," he replied. "Didn't I just see you here yesterday?"

"Yes, sir," I said. "Do you have any jobs here?"

"Didn't I just tell you yesterday that we didn't have any jobs?" he said.

"Yes, sir," I responded, "but I thought maybe someone got fired or resigned."

"Nobody resigned or got fired," Butterball said. "We don't have any jobs."

I thanked him politely and left.

And the next day, I was back, acting as though I was seeing him for the first time.

"How are you doing, Mr. Butterball?"

"What do you want now, young man? I'm busy."

I asked if he had any jobs available.

"Didn't I just tell you yesterday and the day before that we didn't have any jobs?" he replied.

"I didn't know, sir," I said. "I thought maybe somebody died."

"NO ONE DIED. NO ONE GOT FIRED. NO ONE GOT LAID OFF. LEAVE ME ALONE. I DON'T HAVE TIME TO MESS WITH YOU."

"Yes, sir. Thank you," I said.

I left, and again I returned the next day to greet him like I was seeing him for the first time.

"Hello, Mr. Butterball, I'm Les Brown."

"I know what your name is. Go get me some coffee. Make yourself useful."

I did just that. I set about making myself the most indispensable radio station errand boy in the history of broadcasting.

LES BROWN,
from *Live Your Dreams*

JENNIFER HOLLIDAY

❧

come on, effie . . .
sing my song

on opening night of *dreamgirls*
jennifer walked center stage
told em she ain't leavin

all of us in the balcony
were forced to stand
the vibration upon the seats was just that intense

sistah-gurls
hi-five-n
sistah-gurls

we knew exactly what she meant
knew we wouldn't be the ones
runnin out
jumpin ship

not with tenacity
like this
in the family

JACQUELINE JONES LaMON

THE SHINY RED BICYCLE

❦

S A YOUNG BOY growing up in Sanford, Florida, in the 1950s, I dreamed of riding my very own shiny new red bicycle. My granddad never afforded me the pleasure. I was relegated to an old rickety secondhand bike that my Uncle Robert had left from his childhood. His bike was much too big and uncomfortable for my small frame, but I learned to ride it anyway. While all the other kids in the neighborhood rode their brand-new shiny bicycles, I watched with envy.

I can still hear the racing of the big wheels as I sped up and down those dirt roads. My uncle's bike was my real pleasure and an escape to freedom. I felt very independent, at peace and unlimited in my own little space. In the front yards of every house was a tall strong oak tree that shaded the open porches from the hot summer sun. I also dreamed that one day I would build a tree house, but never did. It seems like only yesterday and those streets seem like boulevards to me. Those were the very streets where I played stickball and used two hedges as first and third base. That sleepy little town was still, with an occasional honk of a car horn and children playing in the streets. And little old ladies sat sipping freshly squeezed lemonade as they rocked in their squeaking chairs on their porches, each cooling their body with a paper fan from the church. They fanned themselves as they watched me ride by on that old rickety bike. They had a curious look in their eyes and wondered why I didn't have a new bicycle like the other kids.

Many years went by, but I never stopped dreaming of that new shiny red bicycle. In my mid-twenties in New York City, I finally realized my dream when I purchased my very own shiny new red bicycle. From the moment I stepped on the pedals, I felt powerful, free, and in control again. Each brisk stroke gave me more speed as the wind gushed past my face and ears. It built strength in my legs and pumped oxygen to my heart and lungs. I felt as if I could conquer anything and ride to the end of the earth. I felt like a kid again.

While living in New York and remembering those early years in Sanford, I still ride around town showing off my shiny new red bicycle with my head held high, knowing that I realized my dream.

JON HAGGINS

SELF-DOUBT

❧

ONE DAY a few weeks later, while sitting at home in Mama's chair by myself, thinking about all the new things I was learning, I began to realize that if I tried really hard, I just might actually be able to make a pretty good living at this music thing.

Then, as if on cue, I head the *Voice*.

You know, Barry, you could probably write, arrange, and produce a record all on your own right now . . .

That was the moment I dedicated myself to accomplishing just that. For the next four months, I intensified my self-training and used every contact I knew to try to put something together.

However, in spite of all my focus, energy, and determination, by the summertime, the phone had stopped ringing.

At first I thought maybe I had done or said something

wrong to somebody. I couldn't understand why no one was calling for my services anymore. So here was the next lesson from the School of Real Life: In the music business steady jobs, and therefore regular paychecks, are never guaranteed. And because I didn't have enough knowledge and experience, I did the worst possible thing I could— started to question my own abilities. I had to overcome a lot of self-doubt before I was able to realize that no matter who you are, no matter how good you can be, you're going to hit on some days and miss on others. What you have to hope is you don't miss too many days and eat up the bread you make on the days you do get work. I was determined to keep myself on the plus side of that equation.

B A R R Y   W H I T E ,
from *Love Unlimited*

COMING TO TERMS
WITH THE J-J-JITTERS

❦

M Y FATHER said, "Don't let your mouth get in front of your mind, that's all." It was sage advice, if sometimes difficult for a stutterer to follow. Getting my mouth in front of my mind—words in front of the underlying thoughts—has been a problem for longer than I want to think about, like some threadbare sweater I can't get rid of, can't seem to shake out of my life.

Stuttering is a curious trait, fairly democratic in whom it afflicts (although, for reasons still unknown, it is about five times more common in men than women). And there is no great comfort in knowing the honor roll of power brokers and celebrities said to have been similarly afflicted: Demosthenes. Winston Churchill. Somerset Maugham. Mel Tillis.

For me it's a problem whose roots are indistinct. I can't remember the first time I stuttered, the first time my speech slipped a disk. It was probably a process, a cumulative series of errors. Being of fuzzy origins, my stutter has long been a focal point for friends and acquaintances, a great source of practice, benign and well-meaning, for the shrink in all of them. Everyone has a therapy.

There was the just-slow-down treatment prescribed by my father, a veteran of twenty-two years in the army infantry, twenty-two years spent honing and sharpening his voice into the stentorian instrument it is today. There was the treatment of speech therapists, clinical and compassionate.

And there were therapies of my own. When I was younger, I used avoidance techniques, trading a hard-to-form word for one more easily pronounced. Or there was the ultimate avoidance technique: saying nothing at all.

Stuttering can be a formidable challenge in a society that places a high premium on speaking well. Ours is a culture of sound bites and talking heads, of moral suasion according to the TelePrompTer. If we could elect a president whose strongest asset was a reputation for being a "great communicator," it's clear society looks favorably on the glib.

Society is often less than kind to those who don't speak in the seductive cadences of the network anchor, the commercial pitchman, the world leader. The other side of the conversational coin can mean derision, being made the butt of a multitude of jokes. More of us than will admit, I'm sure, remember the movie theaters of our childhoods, with Porky Pig—that most celebrated stutterer of all— sputtering and twitching his way through a simple sentence, as the audience filled the darkness with gales of laughter, and some of us ached a little inside.

In time, rather than attempt to fight my stuttering, I sought a rapprochement, made an attempt to limit its terrors and to look at it as just a persistent annoyance.

Several years ago, at a journalists' workshop in Tucson, Arizona, I was asked to speak about our group to a reporter from the local public television station. Strangely, when the camera's lights came on, I went into some automatic pilot mode I hadn't experienced before. My responses to the reporter's questions were smooth, polished, relaxed. Afterward she thanked me for the interview. I sensed a quiet satisfaction from her: she thought it had gone well.

The frustrating thing is the difference between such moments—in which I think I could have gone one-on-one with Ted Koppel—and other times, when placing an order at a fast-food restaurant becomes a harrowing experience.

There were other occasions that cut to the heart of the occasional panic, what a speech therapist once called "the j-j-jitters," deliberately repeating the first letter in the word in a written report.

I was more recently invited to speak about journalism to an assembly of students at a southeastern college. It would be, the dean said, nothing stuffy, just a chance to talk shop with the students.

It was not the forum I had envisioned—a small, quiet classroom with a group of eager, friendly undergraduates. The topic had aroused such interest that the location was changed from a twenty-five-seat classroom to a four-hundred-seat auditorium. My talk would be more in the nature of an address to the troops.

My worst fears arose in me that afternoon. I began to speak, mindful of the microphone's ruthless ability to amplify every tic, halt, and breath. My speech went straight to hell. Points so flawlessly made to the mirror in my hotel room sounded lifeless and flat. That fear of public speaking, dodged so blithely in the past, hit with a vengeance. I might have preferred root canal work that day.

This random, unpredictable nature of my stutter is what makes it so annoying—the day-to-day uncertainty of knowing what I'll sound like, who I'll meet to make my sentences jump the tracks.

Perhaps that's why I look for chances to speak in public. Like a novice parachutist or an actor with stage fright, I harbor a desire to push myself into that terror. I know I could fail but I remind myself of the satisfaction of pulling it off.

It happened that way four Christmases ago. I was talking with my father, in one of our brisk discussions on the state of the world. Our chats are often spirited, even heated. We talked about the political climate in America. My father, as always, made his arguments forcefully. But I surprised myself. There in the company of the man who had intimidated me with his eloquence, I brought my arguments home with power and grace. No halting, no reaching for breath, no j-j-jiters. When I finished, he smiled slowly, with a look of joy that went beyond the ambience of the holidays.

"Well . . . okay," he said. "That makes sense." I would have let it go, but his grin persisted.

"You must really like what I said," I suggested.

"I did," he said. "But what I liked even more was the way you said it. You didn't trip once."

If we can remove it from the realm of the cheap laugh, people might see stuttering not as a cartoon disability, but as a conundrum that requires patience, understanding, and a fairly good sense of humor. For me it comes and goes, like a bad cold or a profound case of the blues.

Some speech professionals (perhaps cynics, perhaps realists) say it can't really be cured, its coming and going can't be predicted. But I think it's something you wrestle with and practice at every day. Mostly you put it in its proper place, bottled with the other minor demons of life. When you stumble, you get up, take a deep breath, and start over. You get on with it.

MICHAEL E. ROSS

LESSONS OF THE RIVER

❧

D ESPITE HER LACK of education, Mrs. Blackwell was brilliant and aggressive. Turned down
when she first attempted to register, she
appeared at the courthouse again and again, along with a
few other independent blacks who braved the inevitable
threats until they were added to the rolls. For her imperti-
nence she was told she would never again work in the cotton fields, which was about the only work available. Tall,
dark-skinned, full of wit, and using her own unique version of English, which is more expressive than standard
English, Mrs. Blackwell decided to go to work for SNCC.
She became one of their most effective organizers, a
younger protégée of the "three great women."

During the postmovement years, she worked with
Owen Brooks and Harry Bowie under the aegis of the
Delta Ministry to incorporate Mayersville. This they did

in 1976. The following year she was elected the town's first mayor.

I met Unita Blackwell and her family at her new brick home located not far from the cotton fields where she used to pick.

"All we need now," she said, "is some work here in this place. We're trying to lure a factory."

"Where do the people work?" I asked. There were no businesses in town except for two service stations, two stores, one owned by a black, the other owned by a white, and a new sandwich shop owned by a black man. City hall was a converted church.

"In Greenville, unless they own their own land, or wherever," she sighed.

"But still you like it here?"

"Yes, indeed. I love it. So peaceful this place. And then there is the river. Who wouldn't want to live by the river? I can go anywhere in the world and return here and feel at home by this river.

"I'm only mayor," she reminded me. "I can't work miracles." She certainly can't be expected to, though she herself was something of a miracle. As we spoke, I thought about how her story was like so much of what I had seen in my travels these past ten months: During the civil rights years blacks had achieved the miraculous by kicking open the doors—but once inside, well, there was hardly anything there. It was almost laughable, a kind of special blues truth.

"Let's go drive over to the river," I suggested to her. We got into my car and headed for the gravel road that would take us over the levee. As we were passing the county courthouse, I asked Mrs. Blackwell if she had ever discussed the old days with the county registrar, the woman who had denied her the right to vote until Unita wore her out, and who also lived in Mayersville.

"Oh, yes. I talked with her. She said, 'That's the way we were brought up, Unita. That's the way things were then.'"

As we approached the river, a perfectly pristine scene, I asked, "What did it all mean, do you think?"

"Well, we didn't gain much," Unita admitted. "We changed positions. The river changes positions; it's constantly moving, you know, taking on new routes, cuttin' off old ones. It may not look like it, but it is. Any powerful force will make a change. I suppose what we really gained is the knowledge that we struggled to make this a decent society, because it wasn't. And maybe it still isn't now, but at least we tried. That's history."

TOM DENT,
from *Southern Journey*

A   GIANT   STEP

❧❧❧

WHAT'S THIS?" the hospital janitor said to me as he stumbled over my right shoe.

"My shoes," I said.

"That's not a shoe, brother," he replied, holding it to the light. "That's a brick."

It did look like a brick, sort of.

"Well, we can throw these in the trash now," he said.

"I guess so."

We had been together since 1975, those shoes and I. They were orthopedic shoes built around molds of my feet, and they had a two-and-a-quarter-inch lift. I had mixed feelings about them. On the one hand, they had given me a more or less even gait for the first time in ten years. On the other hand, they had marked me as a "handicapped person," complete with cane and special license plates. I went through a pair a year, but it was always the same shoe, black, wide, weighing about four pounds.

It all started twenty-six years ago in Piedmont, West Virginia, a backwoods town of two thousand people. While playing a game of football at a Methodist summer camp, I incurred a hairline fracture. Thing is, I didn't know it yet. I was fourteen and had finally lost the chubbiness of my youth. I was just learning tennis and beginning to date, and who knew where that might lead?

Not too far. A few weeks later, I was returning to school from lunch when, out of the blue, the ball-and-socket joint of my hip sheared apart. It was instant agony, and from that time on nothing in my life would be quite the same.

I propped myself against the brick wall of the schoolhouse, where the school delinquent found me. He was black as slate, twice my size, mean as the day was long, and beat up kids just because he could. But the look on my face told him something was seriously wrong, and—bless him—he stayed by my side for the two hours it took to get me into a taxi.

"It's a torn ligament in your knee," the surgeon said. (One of the signs of what I had—a "slipped epithysis"— is intense knee pain, I later learned.) So he scheduled me for a walking cast.

I was wheeled into surgery and placed on the operating table. As the doctor wrapped my leg with wet plaster strips, he asked about my schoolwork.

"Boy," he said, "I understand you want to be a doctor."

I said, "Yessir." Where I came from, you always said

"sir" to white people, unless you were trying to make a statement.

Had I taken a lot of science courses?

"Yessir. I enjoy science."

"Are you good at it?"

"Yessir, I believe so."

"Tell me, who was the father of sterilization?"

"Oh, that's easy, Joseph Lister."

Then he asked who discovered penicillin.

"Alexander Fleming."

And what about DNA?

"Watson and Crick."

The interview went on like this, and I thought my answers might get me a pat on the head. Actually, they just confirmed the diagnosis he'd come to.

He stood me on my feet and insisted that I walk. When I tried, the joint ripped apart and I fell on the floor. It hurt like nothing I'd ever known.

The doctor shook his head. "Pauline," he said to my mother, his voice kindly but amused, "there's not a thing wrong with that child. The problem's psychosomatic. Your son's an overachiever."

Back then, the term didn't mean what it usually means today. In Appalachia, in 1964, *overachiever* designated a sort of pathology: the overstraining of your natural capacity. A colored kid who thought he could be a doctor—just for instance—was headed for a breakdown.

What made the pain abate was my mother's reaction. I'd never, ever heard her talk back to a white person before. And doctors, well, their words were scripture.

Not this time. Pauline Gates stared at him for a moment, then said, "Get his clothes, pack his bags—we're going to the University Medical Center," which was sixty miles away.

Not great news: the one thing I knew was that they only moved you to the University Medical Center when you were going to die. I had three operations that year. I gave my tennis racket to the delinquent, which he probably used to club little kids. So I wasn't going to make it to Wimbledon. But at least I wasn't going to die, though sometimes I wanted to. Following the last operation, which fitted me for a metal ball, I was confined to bed, flat on my back, immobilized by a complex system of weights and pulleys. It was six weeks of bondage—and bedpans. I spent my time reading James Baldwin, learning to play chess, and quarreling daily with my mother, who had rented a small room—which we could ill afford—in a motel just down the hill from the hospital.

I think we both came to realize that our quarreling was a sort of ritual. We'd argue about everything—what time of day it was—but the arguments kept me from thinking about that traction system.

I limped through the next decade—through Yale and Cambridge, as far away from Piedmont as I could get. But I couldn't escape the pain, which increased as the joint calcified and began to fuse over the next fifteen years. My leg grew shorter as the muscles atrophied and the ball of the ball-and-socket joint migrated into my pelvis. Aspirin, then Motrin, heating pads, and massages became my traveling companions.

Most frustrating was passing store windows full of fine shoes. I used to dream about walking into one of those stores and buying a pair of shoes. "Give me two pairs, one black, one cordovan," I'd say. "Wrap 'em up." No six-week wait as with the orthotics in which I was confined. These would be real shoes. Not bricks.

In the meantime, hip joint technology progressed dramatically. But no surgeon wanted to operate on me until I was significantly older, or until the pain was so great that surgery was unavoidable. After all, a new hip would last only for fifteen years, and I'd already lost too much bone. It wasn't a procedure they were sure they'd be able to repeat.

This year, my fortieth, the doctors decided the time had come. I increased my life insurance and made the plunge. The nights before my operations are the longest nights of my life, but never long enough. Jerking awake, grabbing for my watch, I experience a delicious sense of relief as I discover that only a minute or two have passed. You never want six A.M. to come.

And then the door swings open. "Good morning, Mr. Gates," the nurse says. "It's time." The last thing I remember, just vaguely, was wondering where amnesiac minutes go in one's consciousness, wondering if I experienced the pain and sounds, then forgot them, or if these were somehow blocked out, dividing the self on the operating table from the conscious self in the recovery room. I didn't like that idea very much. I was about to protest when I blinked.

"It's over, Mr. Gates," says a voice. But how could it be

over? I had merely blinked. "You talked to us several times," the surgeon had told me, and that was the scariest part of all.

Twenty-four hours later, they get me out of bed and help me into a "walker." As they stand me on my feet, my wife bursts into tears. "Your foot is touching the ground!" I am afraid to look, but it is true: the surgeon has lengthened my leg with that gleaming titanium and chrome-cobalt alloy ball-and-socket joint.

"You'll need new shoes," the surgeon says. "Get a pair of Docksides; they have a secure grip. You'll need a three-quarter-inch lift in the heel, which can be as discreet as you want."

I can't help thinking about those window displays of shoes, those elegant shoes that, suddenly, I will be able to wear. Docksides and sneakers, boots and loafers, sandals and brogues. I feel, at last, a furtive sympathy for Imelda Marcos, the queen of soles.

The next day, I walk over to the trash can and take a long look at the brick. I don't want to seem ungracious or unappreciative. We have walked long miles together. I feel disloyal, as if I am abandoning an old friend. I take a second look.

Maybe I'll have them bronzed.

HENRY LOUIS GATES JR.

MARATHON WOMAN

❧

BY NOVEMBER 1993, I was goal weight: 150 pounds. I even got down as low as 148 while running eight-minute miles. I can't tell you what a feeling of accomplishment I had by reaching that weight. I had fulfilled my goal of wanting to be strong and lean and fit and healthy. And I did it in the right way. I literally never felt better. Normally in the old days I would have wanted to celebrate by going out and eating a good meal. But because so much of my life was changing with the discipline it took to get up and work out every day, I wanted to celebrate my fortieth year, not with just champagne toasts but with something that would be symbolic of my health and strength. I decided I would run a full marathon.

At the time I made the decision to do it, I was running about five miles a day. I knew that my mileage would have to increase. [My trainer] Bob [Greene] said, "It's going to require a lot of you. Are you sure you can devote the time, given your schedule? Can you train and do two shows a day?" I said, "No problem."

"No problem" really meant having to rearrange my schedule depending on where I was. That meant sometimes getting up at 4:30 in the morning and running almost every day, no matter what. I remember one day it was pouring rain, and I said to Bob, "Well, can't run today." He said, "Why not?" and I said, "Because my hair will get wet." And he said, "So what, your hair will get wet." I told him, "You know how us black women are about our hair. We can't get our hair wet." He said, "That's nonsense. I'm afraid you will have to get your hair wet. If it's any consolation, mine'll get wet, too." I pleaded, "You don't understand. It's a cultural thing."

He dragged me out. I complained every step of that twelve-mile run up Lake Shore Drive. It poured. I was soaked. My hair got soaked. It was the weekend and [my hairdresser] Andre had the day off. But I managed to dry my hair and make do.

What makes training for a marathon difficult is you have to get the training in no matter what else is going on in your life. And I have a whole other complete, full life. I have the show, and the show must go on. I would do ten or twelve miles in the mornings before shows. I'd save the long runs, fifteen to twenty miles, for the weekends.

I remember the first time I ran twelve miles. I could always determine when I reached twelve, because that's when my legs would start turning to stone. My left leg always felt like a cement block. I'd think, Oh, this must be the twelfth mile, I can feel that little cement block coming on. As I got stronger, I wouldn't feel it until the eighteenth mile. The first day I ran eighteen miles, I was in awe of myself. After the run, I got in the car and went out and drove it. I could not believe it. Eighteen miles is a long way.

We usually ran on the road, single file, with Bob running slightly ahead. I never ran with earphones. I'd sing to myself, meditate, ask myself, What the hell am I doing out here? There were moments when it became surreal and moments when I felt really good that I had the strength to just do it. I felt like a Nike ad.

Well, the big day arrived. And wouldn't you know it, it was pouring rain—a damp, cold rain. And, yes, I was ready for it. I'd been soaked a few times before. It rained the entire four and a half hours that I ran. By the fifth mile, my jacket was so soaked, I took it off and threw it away. It was weighing me down.

I never even felt the first three miles. A lot of runners make the mistake of running too fast in the beginning of the race. They get caught up in all the excitement. This started to happen to me, then Bob said, "You've got to slow down a little." My goal was to run about nine-minute miles and I just ran the first three in under twenty-four minutes. I made the adjustment.

I was wearing the number *40* for my age. I forced myself to drink water every three miles, whether I wanted it or not. I was focused and determined. I spoke to almost no one. When people would shout out my name, I would just nod or raise a hand. We passed monuments and parks and cheering crowds and even a marching band or two. I never looked up. Focused.

The *National Enquirer* had hired two of their guys to follow me. It's the first time I ever talked to a tabloid reporter. They became my checkpoint buddies. I'd ask them, "How far away are we, guys?" They'd say, "Oprah, you're at mile nineteen. Keep going, you look great."

Around the twenty-first mile, I got that old concrete feeling. But at twenty-one, with only five to go, there wasn't a chance I'd stop. When I saw I only had one mile to go, I was overwhelmed with feelings that are to this day difficult to explain.

Flashing through my mind was every year of this weight struggle: every time I prayed to get rid of the weight, every time I tried another diet, every time I'd failed, every time I wanted to be in control of my body and my life but couldn't find the means to do it. Every bad meal, every stuffed feeling, every repressed emotion I was feeling now. I was overcome with exhilaration for what I had done. I could see the finish line. I could actually see the finish line.

Running a marathon is a metaphor for life, I think. It has obstacles, moments when you feel like giving up, when you're tired, overwhelmed. But you keep going. Finally, you can see the finish line. The purpose is clear.

It was a proud and joyful moment, one of the best I've ever had.

OPRAH WINFREY,
from *Make the Connection*

RECIPE FOR TENACITY

❧

S O OFTEN tenacity—stick-to-itiveness, if you pre-
fer—is seen as a matter of cast-iron will. A gnash-
ing of teeth and squinting of eyes in the face of
some formidable obstacle. And sometimes tenacity
requires that. Sometimes to be tenacious means you must
be hard and heavy as a skillet, and able to absorb the blows
of adversity. Sometimes you must be able to withstand
those blows until the opponent, whether it is another
human being or an unfavorable moment in time, wearies
or just goes away. It is the equivalent of a psychic rope-a-
dope. But there is another kind of tenacity. I call it the
tenacity that dances. This tenacity rolls with the punches.
It's water cascading over rock, a Ping-Pong ball bouncing
over rapids. It is the dandelion in a wind storm. While the
dandelion may not come out unscathed, its ability to bow
low—its humility in the face of the storm—prevents it

from being uprooted. Both kinds of tenacity are as real as the palm of your hand and as necessary as the pulsing of your heart. How to find the right balance? There is no infallible formula, but the words of a handful of our most accomplished brothers and sisters provide us with useful markers.

"Learn to take no as a vitamin."—Suzanne de Passe

"By any means necessary."—Malcolm X

"Most folks just don't know what can be done with a little will and their own hands."—Gloria Naylor

"If you lose long enough, the law of averages says that you will succeed."—Doug Williams

"Keep your eyes on the prize, hold on. Hold on."—Sixties civil rights song

"We think we have something to lose so we don't try for that next hill or that next rise. The truth is we have nothing to lose—nothing."—Maya Angelou

"A taste of disappointment is good, because you'll work that much harder so that you never have to have that feeling again."—Michael Jordan

"Belief initiates and guides action."—Octavia Butler

"What they did not realize was that I was stubborn enough to put up with their treatment to reach the goal I have come to attain."—Gen. Benjamin O. Davis Jr.

"The moon moves slowly, but it crosses the town."—Ashanti proverb

ERIC V. COPAGE

Wisdom

A CHRISTMAS CAROL

I'VE GROWN ACCUSTOMED to hearing my father's voice. As I've gotten older, I hear him almost every day. "You're penny-wise and dollar-foolish." "You got champagne tastes, but a water pocket." "Don't believe everything you hear." As my friends and I run into brick walls working our way into adulthood, I am increasingly amazed at the sometimes brutal truth that my father has imparted in his seemingly offhand way.

One Christmas Eve, he and I were working on the furnace of a rental house he owns. It was about twenty below outside and, I thought, colder inside. Tormented by visions of a family-room fire, cocoa, and pampering by my mother (I was home from college), I wanted my father to call it a day and get on with the festivities. After all, it was Christmas.

"We can't," said my father. "This is these people's

home. They should be home for Christmas." He continued wrenching and whanging on a pipe.

I saw an opening. "Exactly. We should be home on Christmas."

He shook his head. "It ain't that simple."

"It'd be simple to call somebody."

"You got a thousand dollars?"

"No. But you do."

"The reason I got it is, I don't give it away on things I can do myself."

A couple of hours later, when we had finished and were loading our tools into the car, he looked at me. "See? That wasn't so hard. But nobody can tell you nothing. That thousand dollars will come in handy. In fact, I'll probably have to send it to you." He shook his head, closed the trunk, and said, "Boy, just keep on living."

"Just keep on living." I often thought it sounded like a threat, but now I see that he was challenging me to see the world as it is and to live in it responsibly. I was like a lot of kids I knew, middle-class, happy, successful at most of what I attempted—but largely at the expense (literally) of my father and the world he created. Now as I contemplate creating a world for his grandchildren, I gain more respect for such accomplishments and the unblinking steadiness it takes.

ANTHONY WALTON,
from *Mississippi*

THE TEN MOST IMPORTANT THINGS TO TELL OUR TEENAGERS

⚜

ADOLESCENCE is trial by fire. Teenagers are simultaneously pulling away from their parents, trying to find out who they are and establish their own values, and fit in with their contemporaries. And that is not to mention the raging hormones wreaking havoc with their body chemistry. It is a time when the wheat is separated from the chaff, when opinions of teachers and society about those on the cusp of taking their place in society begin to solidify. The only thing worse than the hellfire of adolescence is the hellfire of living with an adolescent. It can be a frustrating time for the parent or guardian. You are suddenly looking eye to eye with this human being you have been living with for the past decade and a half. And that is in both the literal and metaphorical sense. He or she is no longer a cuddly infant or a chubby toddler you can cradle in your arms or look down on. This man-child/womanchild is nearly your height, if not taller. And gazing into this adolescent's eyes you are simultaneously staring into your past and into your future. That is what is so frustrating. You want to reach out and prevent her or him from making the mistakes you made, so that, no matter how happy and fulfilling your life is, your child's will be happier and more fulfilling. But teenagers usually won't listen to you. What to do? Don't lecture. Don't hector. Just plant the seeds. Planted in a nourishing soil, these seeds will take root—eventually. You have to have that faith. Here are a few seeds, a few words to live by culled from successful people I have met on my travels. Leave this book open where your resident adolescent might find it. Casually mention this stuff at the dinner or breakfast table. Then have faith that sound thoughts will take root and grow. And remember, the best way to cultivate this tree of knowledge in your children is to plant the seeds in your own garden, and nurture them in your own everyday actions as well.

1. Have Courage. We know that you are sensitive to the judgment of your peers. There is no getting around that. These are your lifelong companions. They were with you in the hospital as you nursed on the bottle; they will be with you in the old age home as your soup is ladled into your bowl. For all practical purposes, they are with you forever. But know that you can select from among them. You needn't grab the first one you happen to see. Set your sights on peers you admire and who bring out the best in you. Set your sights on those who

have a positive attitude and respect for life. Those are the ones worth keeping as friends forever.

2. Dream. A voyage of a thousand miles begins with the first step. What fuels that first step is a vision. A dream. It might be a vision of the ultimate destination. It might be the vision of the wonders of the journey toward a destination. Take time to dream. You needn't complete every journey you plot out on the map, especially at this stage of your life. But get in the habit of dreaming, and of striving toward those dreams.

3. Read. How many times can we say it? How many different ways can we emphasize that reading is fundamental. Reading is power. That was known in pre-emancipation days, which is why teaching African Americans to read was a crime in many states. Reading can give you more than knowledge. Reading can give you more than wisdom. Reading gives the most precious gift: the tools of analysis. It will give you the ability to discern what is of real value. So, read. Continue to read. Reading teaches you how to think. It will also give you a lifetime of inspiration and enjoyment.

4. Speak Up. The squeaky wheel gets the grease. That old saying is true. Speaking up may feel uncomfortable sometimes. Sometimes it is simply easier to be quiet, to let things slide. But then you are letting someone else control your destiny. Never do that. So, speak up when the occasion demands it. No, you may not be

the most popular person in the room at that time. No, you may not always get what you want. But you have made a stand. You will know that you have been true to yourself and fought for what you believe in.

5. Honor Tradition. Align yourself with the best of our traditions. Remember the African kingdoms of Mali, Ghana, Songhay. Remember the great libraries of Timbuktu. Let your actions today honor those traditions, and more contemporary ones, too. Remember, also, that all traditions have a beginning, an original point. Today we take black athleticism in stride. It has become woven into our identity as black people. But it wasn't always so. Years ago, nobody believed in the "natural" superiority of the black athlete. "When we'd walk into the locker room," an old white former boxer recounted to me in the mid seventies, "we weren't intimidated by blacks. On the contrary. We were positive we had the physical superiority to beat them." But that began to change, he said, as more and more black boxers filled the ranks of champions. So, follow in the footsteps of the best of our traditions. But don't be afraid of creating a new tradition of excellence in whatever field you may choose to pursue.

6. Struggle. "That which does not destroy me, makes me stronger." True words. So, do not shy away from the struggles of life. Look at struggle as a gift. Remember what your elementary school teacher said: The car that is used will last longer than the car that is on blocks.

Remember that it is the person who exercises who has the fit body. So, welcome struggle. See it as a fitness routine for character.

7. Make Mistakes. Dare to be stupid. You heard right: Dare to be stupid. Some of the smartest people in the world have gained insights into life or a particular task they have set their minds to by daring to ask the obvious questions. Question others. Question yourself. When you see something you have seen a million times before, dare to ask yourself the most obvious question about it. Renew the world. Dare to be stupid. Make mistakes.

8. Be of Service. The African saying "It takes a village to raise a child," has been mainstreamed into the title of a bestselling book. And it is true: It does take a village to raise a child. And precisely because of that, the child, as he or she matures and benefits from that nurturing, has an obligation to the village. It might be in the form of donating time or money to a charitable organization, or just showing a junior member of the village the ropes in a given situation. Of giving him or her a leg up. So remember that while it takes a village to raise a child, it is the children who sustain the village.

9. Celebrate. There are struggles in life, burdens in life, responsibilities in life. But there is also immense joy in life. So, celebrate life. Celebrate your body by using it wisely and taking good care of it. It is the only

body you will have. Celebrate your mind, because it can take you vast distances. It is possible to expand it infinitely. Celebrate the world around us.

10. Be Yourself. You are unique and irreplaceable.

ERIC V. COPAGE

DOWN-HOME WISDOM

THE COUNTRY preacher glared balefully at the brother who had a habit of correcting his grammar and even his choice of texts for the Sunday sermons.

During this particular sermon he noticed that the know-it-all brother had written down some notes and that he would soon be offering his gratuitous advice. Fixing a baleful eye on the culprit, the preacher ended his sermon by shaking his finger at the offender.

"An' don' you evah fuhgit one thang," he warned. "It ain't the thangs whut you know dat gits you intuh trouble; it's the thangs you know fuh sho' whut ain't so!"

from *Afro-American Folktales,*
edited by Roger D. Abrahams

THE PREMONITION

WHEN I WAS A LITTLE GIRL (about eight years old) I had a recurring dream of a woman that frightened me to no end. In my dreams, the woman was a witch. She did not wear the ugly black dress, or the pointed hat, or the crooked, beat-up witch shoes. She did not cackle like the one in *The Wizard of Oz*, nor did she ride around on a broom. Somehow, though, I knew she was a witch.

She never did anything to harm or frighten me in these dreams. However, for some reason, I was horrified whenever she appeared at night. My heart raced and I began to toss and turn in my sleep. In my dreams, she took me places and spent time with me. She never did anything nor did she make me do anything immoral. She only wanted to be with me.

She looked almost exactly like my mother. The only difference was that she did not have hair or breasts. I eventually saw her bathing in my dreams. That was how I knew that I was with the witch and not my mother. She had been wearing a wig (apparently) so that I would not know who she was. I felt that she was trying to take my mother's place.

The dreams bothered me so much that one night I forced myself to dream up a happy ending. One night after waking up, startled because of the "witch dream," I forced myself to think of something pleasant. When I fell asleep again, I dreamed that I took her to a Disney movie and that she became a nice person. From that night on, I never had the dream again. I never questioned why I had the dream. I guess I was too young to realize that it could possibly have a meaning.

During my last year of college, my mother had suffered from some rare type of skin condition that caused her to break out in a rash all over her body. Her doctors never figured out what it was or how to treat it. By the grace of God, it eventually went away. She lost some of her hair at that time, but it began to grow back. Later, she was diagnosed with breast cancer. As an attempt to stop the spread of the cancer, she had one of her breasts removed. We made it through another storm—or so we thought.

In the fall of 1993, my mother developed a cough that would not go away. While I was working abroad, she went to the doctor for treatment. They treated her for pneumonia and sent her home. After she didn't respond to the treatment, she was further examined. The culprit was determined to be cancer. By now, it had spread all over her body (lungs, bones, and brain). When I returned home to visit her, I saw her for the first time without her head being covered and without her padded bra. At that point, I remembered the dream of the witch. Right then and there, I knew why I had the dream. My mother passed away in the spring of 1994. I now know that God was trying to prepare me for my mother's struggle and death.

MELISSA FLEMING

THREE MANGOES

T HERE WAS ONCE A YOUNG WOMAN on a
Caribbean island. One morning, as she and two
female coworkers walked to town to begin their
job, they came upon an old man. He had a hunchback,
wore ragged clothes, and the leather of one of his shoes
was so worn that it revealed his club foot. Next to him was
a nasty-looking suitcase. He held one filthy hand out, beg-
ging for food.

The young lady's friends all laughed at the man.

"I think he's your type," said the first to the second.

"Au contraire," the second girl responded, nastily. "I
think he rather looks like your last boyfriend." Then they
fell into a fit of hysterics, laughing at their wit and the old
man's fate.

But the young woman looked into the old man's eyes
and felt pity. She reached into her lunch bag and gave the

man half her sandwich. When the sandwich touched the beggar's hand, his hunchback disappeared, he grew six inches taller, and his weather-beaten skin turned a satiny mahogany brown. With his smooth, clean-shaven head and sparkling eyes, he looked like a princely genie.

"Because you had pity on me," he said, "I will give you a choice of one of three gifts." He reached into his suitcase, which was now sparkling like gold, and took out three mangoes. "This mango is for wealth," he said. "One bite of it and money will flow to you like an everlasting stream.

"This mango is for success," he continued. "One bite of it and you can have the job of your dreams, and you will never fail."

He picked up the last mango. "And this mango is for love," he said. "One bite of it and you will spread love and affection throughout the world like a brilliant beacon. Which mango do you want?"

The young woman's friends squawked and cackled like barnyard animals, insisting that she take the mango of success or money.

"Just think of it, you'll never have to work again," said one.

"No, no, take the other," said the second woman. "Just think, you can have the job of your dreams and never fear failing, no matter what!"

The young woman thought for a moment, then reached for the last mango, the mango of love. "My parents have been so good to me," the young woman said. "If I take a bite of it, perhaps I can convey some inkling of how much I appreciate their sacrifices.

"My teachers have been so encouraging to me," she continued. "If I take a bite of it, perhaps I will be able to convey how much I appreciate their faith.

"My friends have been so accepting of me," she added, finally. "If I take a bite of it, perhaps I will be able to convey how much I appreciate their patience." The young woman then cut open the mango and took a juicy bite.

A shadow blotted out the sun, lightning flashed across the sky, and strong winds suddenly kicked up, then just as suddenly died. Everything was as it had been, a pleasant Caribbean morning with the song of birds and the hum of insects. But the princely genie was gone, and at the young woman's feet were the other two mangoes and a note. It read, "You have chosen the fruit of love. The fruit of love bestows wealth beyond measure and success beyond compare. Go in peace and enjoy the fruit of love."

FLORENCE EVANS

THE COMFORTS OF HOME

❧

I'D ALWAYS ENVIED my rich cousins and cursed my own humble surroundings in rural Mississippi. It's not that I had ever met them, but their wealth was a frequent subject of our family dinner conversations. Then one day, those cousins hosted a family reunion, and my mother, father, little sister, and I were flown up.

"What did you see," asked my friends when I returned. "Is it true that they have a car for every day of the week, a television in every room?"

"That and more," I said. "They have more things than you can imagine. They have crystal chandeliers, but hardly a star. They have twelve marble bathtubs, but not a single stream. They have five huge fireplaces, but very little warmth. Everybody has a cell phone, but nobody talks.

"I am thankful for having taken that trip," I said. "Because now I know how rich we really are."

ABRAHAM HARPER

THE BIG YEAR

❧

I T WAS my fiftieth birthday. I was casually lying on a chaise, by the side of the pool, at a friend's home in the country. Later as we casually entered the house, her family surprised me with a gigantic birthday bash, lots of gifts, some of which were practical, like cotton sweaters. Her parents gave me the most memorable gift of all, a membership to AARP (American Association of Retired People). I laughed for twenty minutes.

How did it happen? It seems like only yesterday that I was just forty and fun. Not to say I'm not fun today. But ten years have passed, oh so quickly. "It's too soon. You're too early, come back in ten years," I called out.

Turning fifty sort of sneaked up on me. I looked in the mirror and asked, What happened? A little gray, a little bald, I guess it comes with the territory.

Recently I was riding on a bus, minding my own business, when a three-year-old boy looked up from his father's lap and said, "Don't look at me, bald head." I was taken back by his remark. "Don't be rude, he's not your grandfather," his father remarked. No, thank God I'm not! But after being reminded, I guess I am at the ripe old grandfather's age. I feel fit, energetic, and still sexually appealing at fifty.

This is what growing older means to me:

1. Maturing like a flower that blossoms into the most colorful character.

2. I can watch younger people spread their wings.

3. I can really look in the mirror and like what I see today.

4. I can take advantage of discounts on car rentals and hotel rooms.

5. I can continue having many new experiences and adventures so that I don't have to repeat the same old stories.

6. Having long-time good friends.

At this point in my life I feel free, really free enough to express myself and get away with it. I used to think growing older meant being lonely. But I no longer share that thought. I'm very content with a handful of very special friends to share my life, whether we're talking on the phone, dining out, sharing a movie, or a weekend in the country.

Chronologically age doesn't matter to me. I have friends of all ages and relate to them as just people. It's how I feel about life and I feel *damn* good about it. Several young people in my gym have asked my age. When I tell them fifty, they don't believe me. "How old do you think I am?" I ask. "Forty-something," they reply.

Recently, I was dancing with a friend. As I dipped her to the floor, I yelled, "Not bad for fifty!" "Fifty what?" responded my partner. "Fifty nothing." I quickly sprang up to an erect posture. The secret of being fifty is not looking, acting, or feeling it. I want to stay as vital and look as young as Herbie Hancock.

I don't regret anything I've done, because through each experience I've gained wisdom, whether changing careers in midstream or moving to a new location as I have done over the years. I just counted and realized that I have had four professions during my working years and am looking for another. I don't ever want to stop growing. I've never stood complacent and that's why no grass grows under my feet.

Someone once asked if I wanted to be twenty again. "Twenty, with my knowledge would be ridiculous. No thanks." I don't want to repeat my life, once is enough. I've got a lot of living still to do. I'm going to take AARP in stride and cash in on all the discounts.

JON HAGGINS

FAMILY VALUES

~❊~

IN MY FAMILY'S HOUSE, the dining room table was the center of gravity. Everyone was drawn to the table and once you settled there, it was almost impossible to move away.

Friends and neighbors who dropped by claimed that any time of day or night you could find the Lawrences sitting around the table. Long after we finished eating, we would still be there—my parents, my maternal grandparents, my brother, my sister, and I—three generations under one roof. Generational contrasts and regional differences were reflected at the table: my grandparents' traditional southern diet (fried catfish, cooked cabbage, corn bread, and yams) alternated with our northern dishes (broiled chicken, barely cooked asparagus, and corn on the cob from the local farm stand).

Around the table we would tell stories, relive the day's

events, explore new ideas, and compete for airtime. It was here that we always brought our tales from school, sometimes tales of victory and sometimes miserable laments.

Even though my father was vice president of the local school board, there was much that was taught in school that opposed my family's teachings, and there was much that was not taught that my parents considered central to our education. Through twelve years of school, I remember being asked to memorize the verse of only one black poet, Langston Hughes. Around our table we recited the poetry of James Weldon Johnson, Gwendolyn Brooks, Countée Cullen, W.E.B. Du Bois, Pauli Murray, Paul Laurence Dunbar, Margaret Walker, Arna Bontemps, and Jean Toomer, feasting on the rich language, rhythms, and imagery. We sang the Negro spirituals the way my parents had learned them growing up in black churches and schools in Mississippi. My father insisted that we not confuse spirituals with gospel music, that we honor the "dignity" and power of the simple verse. My parents knew that in our predominantly white school (often we were the only black students in our college preparatory classes) we would never learn about our African-American heritage. Their family curriculum was ritualized, consistent, and intentional.

In my eighth-grade citizenship education class, Miss Shopper—her pale face caked with powder, her eyebrows drawn on with black pencil, wisps of white hair escaping from underneath her red wig—taught us that Abraham Lincoln led the country in the War between the States and that the battle had nothing to do with slavery. Her eyes rested on me—the only Negro child in the class—daring me to challenge her interpretation of history. That evening my parents made the correction. It was "the Civil War," and the institution of slavery was at its very center. And I will never forget my father's rage at discovering the word *barbarian* to describe the Mayan Indians of Central America in my social studies book. He could not resist lecturing us on the "extraordinary" Mayan civilization—its creativity, organization, and resilience—and then immediately sat down at his typewriter to bang out a restrained but angry letter to my teacher. So it was around our own dining room table that we children first heard the dissonance of values and beliefs between our family and our school, and learned that education was not limited to classrooms.

SARA LAWRENCE-LIGHTFOOT, from *I've Known Rivers*

MAKING THE GRADE

❦

I HAD WORKED HARD on that paper. I had spent extra time in the library, foregoing dates, entertainment, recreation, and sleep over the past grueling month, and I thought I deserved an A. So you can imagine how disappointed I was when the teacher handed it back and I saw *B* in fat red marker mocking me from the upper right-hand margin. I approached him after class.

"I deserved an A," I said, pointedly.

He peered at me. There was an owlish quality to him, round horn-rimmed glassed, tweed jacket with elbow patches, close-cropped beard flecked with gray. The hair on his head was also close-cropped, graying and receding. If you placed a pipe in his hand and hounds at his feet he'd look like a sepia-tinted caricature of a British scholar—you know the kind: always vaguely squinting, vaguely buck-toothed men who punctuate their sentences with "'Wha? Wha?"

But in motion, Mr. Pierson was no tea-sipping denizen
of the ivory tower. And while he was neither tall nor mus-
cular, he still maintained some of the swagger that made
him one of the most fearsome members of a gang he used
to run with in his youth—the Jolly Stompers. He shared
all kinds of tales about his teenage years with us, but left
to our imagination how the gang came by its name.

Mr. Pierson had grown up in the school of hard knocks
on the worst corner in Philadelphia, where through the
grace of God and a chance encounter as a fourteen year
old, he met a man who grandly announced to him one day,
"I am going to change your life." The man paid for Mr.
Pierson to have remedial tutoring and put him into one of
the best eastern boarding schools. Mr. Pierson had struggled and flourished. For reasons he kept to himself, after
graduating from Yale, he decided not to take the fast track
for the upper echelon of some multinational corporation.
He chose instead to teach high school English in a small,
black Atlanta suburb.

He continued to peer at me, this man, this coagulate of
contradictions. At first I thought that he was deciding
whether he could take me on, a forty-year-old former gang
member against a junior in high school. I wasn't afraid.
He may once have been a member of the Jolly Stompers,
but I am a big guy. Six foot three, 215 pounds. I wrestled
and played football. I wasn't afraid of getting physical if it
should come to that—the two of us alone in his classroom.

Turns out he was sizing me up, but in a different way
than I had suspected. He gently took the paper from me,
took out a felt pen, scratched out the B, and wrote *This is*

Michael's paper. He got an A. He then went to his grade book, changed the B to an A, and without a word left the room.

The next day in class he gave a pop quiz. He had everyone in the class correct one another's quiz, but he took mine. When he handed it back to me, he had duly noted what I had gotten wrong, but there was no grade. "Fill it in with whatever you want," he said.

This went on and on with tests, quizzes, and homework throughout half the semester. "Fill it in with whatever you want." At last, near the first marking period, I grabbed him after class. "So, how am I doing?" He looked at me quizzically. "I thought you were going to be in charge of evaluating that." I felt a hotness rising within me, partially borne of frustration, partially of anger, partially of embarrassment. I knew where he was going. "But how am I really doing?" I asked. He looked at me levelly. "I told you near the beginning of the semester. But you didn't believe me. You didn't want to hear it. You knew better. So, now you tell me."

"It's not that I though that I knew better," I protested, "I just knew that I worked too hard to get only a B."

He took an enormous breath that seemed to be more like a sigh. It was as if he were recalling an ancient memory. "I know you thought you deserved an A. And I am sympathetic to that. I could see that you worked hard. I applaud that. And if there were a place to grade for effort on papers, you would have gotten an A. But the grade reflects results, not effort. Your paper was a B. A good strong B, but a B nonetheless. Do you want me to grade you, or do you want to continue grading yourself? With me, you will be graded fairly, and in a way that prepares you for life."

I'm not going to lie to you. I did think about what it would be like to grade myself, to have one class in which I could have a guaranteed A, ironically an effortless way to jack up my grade point average. I also wondered if he would really let me do it. He sat behind his desk and began doing schoolwork as I pondered all this.

"Yes, I would like you to grade me," I blurted out. He smiled and asked me to pull up a chair next to him. Night came and we were still going through the old papers and exams. He explained in detail why he would have given me certain grades. The next paper, I worked hard, but also with intelligence. I knew what was expected, what to expand on, and what to cut out. When we got our papers back, my chest was so constricted, I could hardly breathe. It seemed to take forever for my five typewritten pages to make their way back to me. And when they arrived, I saw in the upper right-hand corner a big fat A winking at me. It had a circle around it. And you know what? I deserved it.

AS TOLD TO ERIC V. COPAGE

THE INSIDE LIGHT

NOW TAKE FRIENDSHIP, for instance. It is a wonderful trade, a noble thing for anyone to work at. God made the world out of tough things, so it could last, and then He made some juice out of the most interior and best things that He had and poured it around for flavor.

You see lonesome-looking old red hills who do not even have clothes to cover their backs just lying there looking useless. Looking just like Old Maker had a junk pile like everybody else. But go back and look at them late in the day and see the herd of friendly shadows browsing happily around the feet of those hills. Then gaze up at the top and surprise the departing sun, all colored-up with its feelings, saying a sweet good night to those lonesome hills, and making them a promise that he will never forget them. So much tender beauty in a parting must mean a friendship. "I will visit you with my love," says the sun. That is why the hills endure.

ZORA NEALE HURSTON,
from *Dust Tracks on a Road*

UNCONDITIONAL LOVE

❧

WHEN I AM AROUND my friends I feel *good*. I feel *secure*. Our friendship is based on something that is completely unspoken: trust. And that trust, combined with years of experiences together, has forged a bond of understanding and unconditional love. And that gives *them* the freedom to be truthful with me. They know that I might not like what they have to say—but they also know that I won't cut them off for telling me the truth.

I decided early on that it wasn't the number of people in my posse that counted but the quality of those people. I couldn't think, act, sing, or be myself if I were going to be with people who dug into me. Now, I am not saying that it was always easy to walk away from people. It's never clearcut. Every life has people who amuse you with good times—on the surface—but who prick holes in your self-

W I S D O M

confidence by putting down your ideas or making off-handed comments that shoot right for your Achilles' heel. And just when you think, Dag, I don't want to hang with this, boom, you end up going out dancing, sitting by the ocean, sharing some laughs. But what I realized with those people in my life was that a lot of the negativity stuck. And getting it unstuck took energy. The superficial fun wasn't worth it, because deep down I had been poked.

So I decided, early on, that if I was going to be Queen Latifah, feeling worthy and good about myself so that I could be my best, then I had only one choice about the company I kept. It would be only with the people who brought out the best in me. I had to lose the rest. It was not always an easy choice, but I am proud of it. Never do I find myself wasting time with people. Instead, I have the hours—and the head—for those I can count on for love and truth.

QUEEN LATIFAH,
from *Ladies First*

RECEIVING IN ORDER
TO GIVE

❧

I LEARNED this lesson the hard and vivid way. When I
was a young teacher at Tuskegee Institute in
Alabama, from 1968 to 1970, I was often invited to
preach in the pulpits of small, rural, black Baptist
churches in Macon County—tiny, hardscrabble places
that rejoiced in such mellifluous names as Mount Pisgah,
Zion's Hill, St. John of Patmos, and Ebenezer. In these
places they paid the preacher by taking up a "love offering" for him immediately after the sermon, and it became
something of a referendum on preacher and sermon alike.
The people were usually generous-hearted, and grateful
for the attentions and efforts of a young man new to the
ministry and to them. Early on, I refused these offerings
on the grounds that these poor people and their poor
church needed the money more than I did since I had a
decent salary from the institute, after all, and it was my

pleasure to give. In fact, it made me feel quite morally superior to decline these gifts, and to give them back. I knew even then that giving was essentially an expression of power, and that it was power perhaps more than charity, philanthropy, or stewardship that caused me to refuse the offerings of the people.

In the nicest possible way I boasted of my practice to the formidable dean of women at Tuskegee, who had become a friend and mentor, and was herself a preacher's widow. She was not impressed. In fact she upbraided me without mercy for my arrogance. "Who are you," she thundered, "to refuse to accept the gift of these humble people? You have given insult by refusing to let them do what they can for you." I, for a change, was speechless. She then concluded with a phrase that will remain with me all of my days: "You will never be able to give until you learn how to be a generous receiver." Jesus himself could not have put it better, and he was perhaps easier on the rich ruler than Dean Hattie Mae West Kelly was on me. Never again did I refuse to accept a love offering, and it was then, I think, that I first got an inkling as to what wealth was about.

PETER J. GOMES,
from *The Good Book*

BEARING WITNESS

⟋⟍

I HAD JUST FINISHED giving a talk at a New York City middle school, a talk about my job as an editor with a major national magazine, when one of the students came up to me. I had been warned before my talk that he was a smart aleck and would likely be disruptive. And indeed, he had lived up to his reputation, but not disrespectfully so. When he had interjected his comments—wise cracks, really—the teacher tried to silence him, while I, in a way that would not contradict the authority of the teacher, tried to listen to what the young man had to say. More often than not his comments had the kernel of a slashing truth or insight. The way he made his comments may have been inappropriate, but what he had to say was interesting.

There was a sullenness about the young man, but by what I could gather, that sullenness did not prevent him from being the heartthrob of the class. He had a dark, satiny complexion, and the hint of an adolescent mustache. And when he wanted to flash it, he had a winning smile. I noticed that virtually every girl gave him a furtive but admiring glance as they filed out of the room.

He stood before me—all of thirteen or fourteen years old—dressed in the baggy hip-hop style of the day, with a carriage that hadn't lost the buoyancy of childhood nor acquired the gravity of an adult. He didn't seem to have any psychological demons nor domestic dramas. Yet, as he had told me during my talk, he was doing poorly in school. And seemed proud of it.

"I hate white people," he said, picking up where we had left off in the discussion part of my talk, "and all I'm learning in this place is white stuff. Why should I have anything to do with people who have oppressed and still oppress my people?"

I looked at him, measuring my approach. I had been that young man thirty years ago. I had asked the same question. I didn't want him to take as long as I had to find the answer.

I tendered the following question gently. "Did Charlie Parker," I asked him, "look at the saxophone and say, 'I'm not going to touch that because it was created by a white man'? No, he took it, mastered it, and used it to bear witness."

The young man did not let off with a wise crack. He did not crack a smile. I went on. "Did Ralph Ellison look at the novel and say, 'I'm not going to touch that because it was created by a white man'? No, he took that literary form, mastered it, and used it to bear witness."

I could feel the young man was with me. "Did Romare Bearden or Henry O. Tanner look at the canvas and say, 'This is the invention of the white man, so I am not going to touch it'? No! They took the canvas, put paint on it, like white people had done, but used it to bear witness to our people."

I thought I saw a light in the young man's eyes. He may not have been agreeing with me, but at least he was understanding. I then let loose with the big gun, Malcolm X, revolutionary icon for at least two generations of young black men. Surely, no one would accuse Malcolm of being an Uncle Tom, of selling out.

"Did Malcolm X look at the English language and say, 'This is the language of the white man, so I won't have anything to do with it'? No! He took that language and put a leash around it. And he made it sit when he said sit. He made it jump with he said jump. He made it roll over when he said roll over. And then he took that language across the water, to England, where they had invented that language. And it was there, during the Oxford University debates, that he showed them who was now master of that language. And what did Malcolm do with this language he'd mastered? The young man nodded and completed my thought: "He used it to bear witness," he said.

"Our forefathers and foremothers used the whole world around them to bear witness to our struggles," I said. "They used the world around them to bear witness to our triumphs. To bear witness to our goodness."

* * *

About a year and a half later, I was giving a talk at a New York City high school. It was early December and I was talking about Kwanzaa. After my talk, on my way out of the building, I bumped into the young man. He had grown, it seemed, a good six inches, and the hint of a mustache was replaced by stubble from shaving. Lots can happen in a year and a half.

I asked him how he was doing in school, and he told me that he was enjoying his studies. It was marking period and he pulled out his report card to show me. Straight As. He said that he was excited about the prospect of being college bound.

You may ask, how can a young person, especially a young man in the throes of adolescent rebellion, turn from a failing student to an honor student so quickly. It's not that he wasn't smart enough, you might say, but are we really to believe that such a change in *attitude* can happen.

Well, first of all, I can tell you that the young man almost certainly did not change because of what I said, because of that one conversation. But I can tell you that change he did, and apparently suddenly. Who can explain it? These things do happen. I can bear witness.

ERIC V. COPAGE

TIME FLIES

WISDOM consists of seeing the long-term conse-
quences of your actions. Sometimes it is better
to face the immediate effects, no matter how
unpleasant, rather than seek refuge in momentary safety or a
good feeling that might be illusionary. For instance, there
was once a thief who was fleeing from the police. He ran up
the stairs of a very tall building, the police in hot pursuit.
When he finally arrived on the building's roof, he took one
last look at his chasers, then jumped. The astonished cops
gawked at the tumbling man. As he fell, they didn't hear him
scream, they didn't hear him call out for God's forgiveness. As
he fell they only heard his calm voice, growing fainter and
fainter, echoing off the surrounding buildings, saying, "So
far, so good. So far, so good. So far, so good. So far, so good . . ."

AS TOLD TO ERIC V. COPAGE

RECIPE FOR WISDOM

⁓❖⁓

W HAT IS WISDOM? Some may say wisdom is the accumulation of knowledge—rote memory of the dates, facts, figures, and other minutia of the everyday world around us. Some say wisdom does not lie in this world but in the ethereal realms— that true wisdom has nothing to do with the accumulation of facts, but with achieving a closer relationship with the original spiritual source, and that we will not achieve true wisdom until we cross over to that other world. Some say wisdom is simply being aware of our animal needs and practical desires and accommodating them. The Solomons among us might say that the truth about wisdom is a blend of all of the above—and more. The Solomons might say that wisdom is familiarizing ourselves with the granite and silk of this world, but then connecting that knowledge with a higher power. That we should acknowledge our baser instincts, but then strive to rise above them. That true wisdom is some blend of our parents chiding us to always wear clean underwear and the theology of the Upanishads. Here is a brief sampling of steps that may lead to wisdom, no matter how you define it, made by friends and strangers and garnered from graffiti on walls and from books, magazines, and talk shows.

1. Lay out tomorrow's breakfast tonight.
2. Know who you are.
3. Know that you are more than that.
4. Floss.
5. Make "to do" lists.
6. Treat your signature as your most precious possession.
7. Know where you come from.
8. Know where you are going.
9. Eat your vegetables.
10. Read the fine print.
11. Use sunblock.
12. Question everything. Think!
13. Work/play, orkp/layw, rkpl/aywo, kpla/ywor, play/work.
14. Listen . . .
15. Reflect.

ERIC V. COPAGE

Faith

EVERY WOMAN HAS A CALL

IN THE BIBLE, the apostle Paul talks about learning contentment.

> . . . I have learned, in whatsoever state I am, therewith to be content. I know both how to be abased, and I know how to abound: every where and in all things I am instructed both to be full and to be hungry, both to abound and to suffer need. I can do all things through Christ which strengtheneth me.
> —Philippians 4:11-13.

We live in a society that tells—promises—us that material things breed contentment. If we possess and own, if we satisfy our desires, we will be happy. And if we don't, we'll be miserable. If you don't drive the right kind of car, you are pitiful. If you don't sport the latest Air Jordans, the phattest gear, you're considered a Herb. If you don't have a lot of money, you're weak. And if you don't have a man, you're not a complete woman. The media tells us this. Sometimes our friends suggest as much, and often our parents may even make us feel inadequate. And we tell ourselves these same lies. We run after things as if our whole being depended on it.

I know a lot of people who think that this world owes them something. It's an easy attitude to come by. I am guilty of having felt that I deserve my real friends after giving myself to people who took advantage of me. That I warrant success and fame and all of my dreams because I've worked my ass off and made a lot of money for a lot of people. I have even felt that I am due some heavy compensation for all the pain that came from losing those close to me and losing myself. Shouldn't I get true love? Don't I deserve a break? I have caught myself thinking.

Life doesn't owe me—or anyone—a thing.

Everything that you are, everything that you can be, starts inside of you and it starts with God. Nothing can take the place of a great friendship, a true love, or a big brother. There isn't a deal, a contract, a car, a bank account, or a promise that can mend a broken heart or make you believe in yourself.

The one thing that keeps me grounded is knowing that God created me in Her image. She made me to be just like Her. My capabilities and my possibilities are endless. I have the potential to create, to heal, to comfort, to love, to be the best me I can possibly be. Once you realize what you can do and who you are, you can relax in the confidence of being you. In *Conversations with God,* Neale Donald Walsch says that life is not like school, where you have to learn, but it is a process of experiences, where you ultimately remember who you are. You are given what you need for life at birth, and you spend this life remembering what was placed in you, remembering who you are. But what reminds you?

You.

You can't find out who you are and what you're made of if you're too afraid to look hard at yourself. I would be lost if I hadn't stared myself down. I looked at myself through the eyes of my mother and God. And at times I didn't like what I saw. But I was the only one with the power to change it. I had to wake myself up, slap myself in the face, and realize who I was—and who I wasn't. And be me.

And now I just keep reaching for that mark. Every day I have to remind myself of my core.

As Queen Latifah, I have had so many people slap images and labels on me. People have expectations of who they think I am or who they think I should be. But I am not just the outer covering that people see. I don't have to wear a sign that says I AM QUEEN LATIFAH for people to treat me with respect. I command it. And I don't need Queen Latifah to be a queen. All I need is to be myself.

To get to the point of being myself, though, I had to go through a whole bunch of years of being something *other* than myself. I went through the tomboy stage. The not-feeling-good-about-my-body stage. The awkward-sex stage. The giving-up-my-sex-for-money stage. The running-wild stage. The doing-drugs stage. The wanting-to-die stage. And I realized they were extremely valuable stages to go through. They were part of life's process.

As I continue to grow in my queenliness, I've learned that there is no greater quality than contentment. It is the mother of peace. But the apostle Paul isn't talking about *getting* contentment, he's talking about *growing into* it. He's saying that it comes from what we have *within* us, not *around* us. I can be content in every situation, as the apostle Paul says, because I know that each experience, each hardship, each joyous occasion is simply preparing me for the next level, the next layer of me. I ride it out and see where it takes me.

The power to be who I wanted to be was—and is—with me the whole time. We all have the power to be the person we set our sights on being. We have the power to change our lives so that we are at peace. It is just a matter of using that power in the right way. *Power*. The word goes with being a queen. The key is not to rule others but to reign over yourself. As free people, we have the power to constantly reevaluate and remake ourselves. We are always evolving.

But don't confuse having the power with controlling every situation in your life. You can only control the way you respond to situations; you can't always control events. Do you fly off the handle, throw tantrums, and bug out every time something inconvenient or bad happens? Or do you ride it out, knowing that "this too shall pass"? Do you view every situation as a problem? Do you bitch and complain all the time? Or do you make the best of everything?

Contentment, peace, starts within. Whom do you see when you look at yourself? A person who is always worried, nervous, and anxious? Or a person who is made in the image of God?

There is plenty in life that our power can't touch. When [my brother] Winki died, it was the most painful, tragic thing ever to come into my life. For the longest time, I threw energy into wanting to bring Winki back. I wanted my mom to heal. I wanted peace for my father. I couldn't stop the pain. I was self-destructive. My hand was a fist, and I could not recover from the grief.

But the time of my brother's death was also a period of intense evolution for me. That day, sitting in church, a year after Winki's death, I achieved a milestone. I had carried on—lived, loved, and made an award-winning album—through—and because of—unimaginable pain.

I take nothing for granted anymore. I am grateful for every blessing in my life.

QUEEN LATIFAH,
from *Ladies First*

THE CHAMPION

I AM NOT A QUITTER. I will fight until I drop. It is just a matter of having some faith in the fact that as long as you are able to draw breath in this universe, you have a chance.

CICELY TYSON

SWIMMING LESSONS

❦

I HAD TAKEN SWIMMING LESSONS when I was in my early teens, having only learned the backstroke. I didn't practice because there wasn't a pool at my disposal. On three occasions when I was in my twenties and thirties, I almost drowned in Rio de Janeiro and Hawaii. So at the age of forty-nine, when a friend told me about a New York City recreational facility that only cost twenty-five dollars per year, I was ecstatic. The Romanesque-style building was originally built as a bathhouse at the turn of the century. New York City had spent six million dollars renovating the entire building. The amenities included a full-service gym with all-new equipment, a shower, and a pool. After carefully investigating the facility, I joined immediately. I figured this was a fabulous opportunity finally to learn and practice swimming.

After observing several athletic, stylized swimmers, I

began timing their movement through the water. Their strokes had a rhythm and a count as in dance. I began counting and stroking across the width of the pool while my friends swam the length. I shared a dreadful fear of panicking then drowning in water where I couldn't touch the bottom. Therefore, I'd stand only in the shallow end.

One day a young man who'd been observing me for weeks suggested that I try to swim the length. He suggested that he'd swim along to give me moral support. I emphatically stated, "No way." The water was fourteen feet deep on the other end and there was no way I could swallow it. After several days of encouraging me, he finally convinced me to charge ahead. I foolishly believed that he would accompany me, so I set out with a brisk backstroke up the length of the pool. When I arrived at the opposite end, he was still standing in the shallow water. After I reached the other end and relaxed, I realized this was the best way to learn and to build confidence.

Two days later, as I was floating on my back, suddenly my entire body was submerged and I couldn't rise to the surface. It was like the commercial where the little old lady fell on the floor and yelled, "I've fallen and I can't get up." I, too, panicked and called out for help. Everyone in the pool including the lifeguard thought I was fooling around. They looked at me and said, "Yeah, right." Something suddenly came over me. I relaxed and surfaced, then floated away and realized that I had saved myself. From that day forward I've never been afraid of deep water.

JON HAGGINS

NOT MY TIME

✦

FEW EVENTS alter our thoughts and actions as
drastically as when we experience that unexpected
brush with death.

I'd been at my new job one month when the events of a
rainy October day changed my life. During lunch break
I'd planned to travel across town to make an appearance at
a local leadership function.

Early morning drizzle made for slick driving conditions.
I had a plan. I'd go to the leadership meeting, then grab a
bite to eat on the way back to the office. Sounded like a
wonderful plan, that is, until one of those "unexpected"
incidents happened. Often times we plan things without
giving consideration to extenuating circumstances.

I traveled west toward my destination. As if in slow
motion, what happened next played like slides from a
home movie. A vehicle traveling to my right peripherally

caught my eye. I remember thinking, Damn, that car's not going to be able to stop. I gently eased my foot from the accelerator in an attempt to avoid a direct hit with the driver's side of the oncoming vehicle. In doing so I was on a collision course with the concrete expressway overpass.

So much was running through my mind. I'd spent the better part of my life trying to prove, to others, that I controlled my destiny. Yet I hurtled smack dab into the middle of a situation over which I had no control. Saying my life flashed before my eyes puts an implausible spin on events; however, this was real. I was in a pragmatic vortex out of control and unsure of the outcome.

In an attempt to brace for obvious impact, I remember grabbing the wheel so tight my fingernails dug into the palms of my hands. Visual impressions remained long after the accident. I asked God to comfort my family, to help them to deal with whatever the outcome. To put it bluntly, I thought I was going to die. In a moment and blinking of an eye it was over. A passerby ran to my aid. My crinkled-up car, perched against tons of immovable concrete, bore chilling reminders of how quickly things can change.

I know it's no coincidence a nurse ate lunch across the street at McDonald's that day. I know God disperses angels, at the appropriate time. What else could explain her being there taking my vitals, talking to me, keeping me calm until emergency workers arrived.

Emergency personnel arrived quickly. As medical personnel masterfully outfitted me for extraction, a back and neck brace became props. Taped to the backboard, physically and emotionally helpless, I struggled pointlessly against my now trapped state. I'd not felt as alone in my life.

As I continued to struggle against my bandage trap, I told myself I could close my eyes and not open them ever again. My struggles would be over. Flat on my back, head and neck immobilized, eyes tight, the Holy Spirit spoke to my heart, saying, "Be still, Theresa, and know I'm God." With that it started to rain. Droplets of rain, what I now call tears of the Lord, fell gently upon my face. I opened my eyes, seeing my surroundings as never before.

I'd spent all my life fighting for one thing or another. At age seven, the youngest of nine, it was something as simple as a quiet place to call my own. At fifteen it was proving I was a good mother, though society already had me labeled. At twenty it was proving I could make it in college—against the odds. At thirty there were internal fights between morality and immorality. At thirty-three, I heard my savior say, "Be still." However, I had to be lying flat on my back and helpless to hear it.

I don't take the accident lightly. That day God wrapped me in His loving arms, assuring me He wasn't through with me yet. There is much work for me to do. I'm reminded daily that rainy October day simply was "not my time."

T. C. MATTHEWS

THE PEACEMAKER

G OD really does protect babies and fools.

A writer by profession, I recently took off some time to teach in an impoverished Washington, D.C., neighborhood where I once attended Sunday school. I was assigned a fifth-grade class, and when I saw one student in particular on my list I gasped for air—for strength really. Tutoring at this school previously had taught me who the biggest troublemakers were and Phillip was the ringleader of them.

My first instinct was to sit him up front next to me, so I did. I designated him my special helper since he was two years older than most of his classmates. I figured his leadership just needed a little guidance. Silly me.

Each month, teachers selected a student leader—Most Studious, Most Helpful, Best Peacemaker, Most Conscientious, et cetera. I selected Phillip as our peacemaker despite his reputation as a troublemaker because he hadn't caused any trouble in our class during these first six weeks in school. Besides, I wanted to give him a chance at something new.

I talked to him about making peace rather than war and breaking up fights instead of instigating them. But, in my noble efforts, I neglected to clear my intentions with the principal. During the student leaders ceremony, she could not disguise her surprise and dismay when he strutted across the stage to shake her hand and receive his Peacemaker certificate. All around the auditorium students snickered and teachers shook their head in embarrassment at my naivete.

After school, the principal scolded me and questioned my judgment. "Everyone knows he's anything but a peacemaker!" she fumed. "I'm trying to show him he can turn that around," I muttered. We would have to discuss my poor judgment later, she concluded.

In the following weeks, his classmates set out to prove what an error I'd made. He seemed to love the challenge, slipping and sliding between trouble and peace for weeks. One day he'd be hauled into the principal's office for bullying someone, the next day he could be seen breaking up a fight.

When spring arrived, I designated him caretaker of the new class plants so his classmates could see another side of him.

At the year-end awards ceremony, I almost cried when the principal called him to the stage to receive the Most Improved Student award. She acknowledged that he'd been in twelve fights the previous school year and only two this year. She encouraged him to continue his efforts and asked the school to keep him encouraged, as well.

I took a picture of him hugging the principal, and smiling down at his very special award. God must have been smiling on all of us that day.

SONSYREA TATE

THE COMMUNION CUPCAKE

◦❈◦

F OR ME, chocolate is the *M* word: It is mouth-
watering, it is marvelous, it's *mmmmm* so delicious. The way the Dr. Seuss character, Sam I Am,
came to feel about green eggs and ham, I feel about chocolate. I could eat it anywhere, hot or cold, in candy bars, on
top of cars, in drinks, cakes, and pies, brownies, ice cream,
and gelatos. Since I usually have some form of chocolate
several times a week, if not every day, it made the perfect
item for my siblings to tease me with. It also made the perfect pleasure to give up for Lent. And during one recent
Lent season, not too many years ago, my sister's jibing and
the strictures of Lent met at a lunatic juncture, where I
was put to the test.

I had thought about giving up chocolate for many a
Lent. But when it came to choosing between giving up
chocolate for forty days or giving up sex, I always chose

sex. Just kidding. I choose neither sex nor chocolate. I kept them off my Lent list. I chose giving up alcohol, or exercising, which I really do enjoy (thank goodness, since I love chocolate so), or not going to the movies or watching television.

But recently my older sister dared me to give up chocolate for Lent. She didn't think I could do it and I can't pass up a dare. In games of truth or dare I always choose dare, not only because I am a very private person, but because I enjoy the thrill of it. Once, when our parents took us for a vacation in Hawaii, my sister and I stole away to the top of a big rock overlooking a small lake. She was eleven and I was nine. She dared me to jump off. I did, just barely clearing the rocks, landing maybe twenty feet later (it's hard to gauge, using my child's eye) with a painful flop that stung and dazed me. I have various scars that attest to the other daring dos of my childhood.

This is what my sister was playing on when she challenged me to go without chocolate for Lent. I was at her house being auntie to her two children, when she said it as a joke (I think). But I took her on.

Day 1: So far, so good.

Day 2: No withdrawal symptoms—yet.

Day 7: Delirium tremors set in. (Just kidding!)

Day 12: I had a dream last night. I was rolling among the satiny folds of chocolate frosting, which rose and fell like the hills in the countryside. I awoke with a tummy-ache.

Day 16: Reading a scratch and sniff book to my four-year-old nephew. The illustration is of a yuletide living room. We scratch the peppermint candy, put our nose to the page to take in the peppermint scent. The same with the Christmas tree. When we scratch the cup of hot chocolate, I almost go into a swoon. My nephew has to restrain me from gnawing on the page.

Day 22: Saw a child eating a Hershey's—and want to mug him for it.

Day 28: Is lusting in your heart for food the same as eating it? A theological question I will ponder trying to get my mind off chocolate.

Day 30: See TV documentary on a people who eat chocolate-covered ants. Yum!

Day 38: In my mind's eye, everything I eat is covered with chocolate—the hamburger I had for lunch, the ketchup is chocolate. The mashed potatoes have chocolate gravy. I seemed to slather white chocolate on my toast this morning. Two more days. I'm almost there.

On the thirty-ninth day I have a feeling of great personal triumph. And this time there are no scars or injuries from having—almost—succeeded with this dare. I chat with my elderly neighbor over the backyard fence. She is recently widowed and her children scattered to the winds—one to another part of the country, two to another part of the world. Her husband was the center of her life and she is having a difficult time adjusting to her solitude and invites me over to chat. How could I say no?

Her living room is overheated and is a little stuffy, having not yet been opened up from the winter. We sit on the plastic-covered couch, just the two of us. She talks about her life, her late husband, the transition she is struggling to make in life. She is not a great storyteller. She is not really used to relating to people outside her immediate family.

Suddenly, or as suddenly as an eighty year old with arthritis can, she stands up and ambles out of the room. "Do you need any help?" I ask, "Oh no," she croaks back, returning with two small plates, a chocolate cupcake with a single candle on each. It is her birthday.

"I know how much you like chocolate," she says. I consider telling her that she had been mistaken about my love of cupcakes, but I don't think she would believe me. I consider telling her the truth, that I had given up chocolate for Lent, and I figure that she would understand. But looking at her wrinkled hand offering me the plate, I feel her loneliness. But I have doubts. Am I just looking for an excuse not to cross the finish line of my resolve? Do I truly feel that it would be a religious failing not to eat chocolate before the completion of Lent? Do I really feel for her loneliness and want to make what, at her age, could be her last birthday, the very best I can? Or, indeed, am I just looking for an excuse to punk out and eat the cake.

Torn between my possible motivations, I ask myself what would Jesus, Muhammad, or Moses do? I conclude that they would have had mercy, set pride aside, and eaten the cake.

I light the candles and sing a gospel version of "Happy Birthday" to her, and she giggles like a child. I wish her "many more" birthdays, and we blow out the candles. The cupcake is delicious—dark, moist, and light. It doesn't need a glass of milk and the homemade frosting was the texture of satin. As I put the last morsel in my mouth, a strange thing happens. I look at my plate and see only the usual crumbs. But in my mouth, in my soul, I have the sudden exaltation I remember as a child after having eaten a Communion wafer.

AS TOLD TO ERIC V. COPAGE

NOW OR NEVER

❧

IT WAS A WEDNESDAY night in May 1960 that
changed my life. I went to bed, sank into my bunk,
when all of a sudden out of the bleak stoneblock
nowhere down the hall from some other's inmate radio I
started to hear this song. I'd heard it before, I don't know,
twenty-five, thirty times, but it never hit me like it did
that night. It was of all people, Elvis Presley! The song?
"It's Now or Never."

It became a personal message, meant only for me. "Stop
wasting your time, Barry," it said. "When you get out you
better change your ways. It's now or never!"

I sat up in my cell bed and right then and there took an
oath that I would do just that—change my life.

The next morning when I woke up everything around
me looked and felt just a little bit different. I held onto the
feeling until three months later, in August, when my court

hearing finally came up. I was still determined to turn things around. Step number one was to get out of there. My immediate goal was to make sure I didn't go from Juvenile Hall to Soledad.

I was in the little holding room outside two courtrooms with all the other juvenile "bad" boys. Some went into this one where a certain judge was and some went the other way. Everybody who went to the left was sent up. They'd come out and say, "Oh, man, I got twenty-two months . . ." Everybody who went to the right got a free pass home. Then my name was called—Barry White—and the man sent me to the left! My stomach flip-flopped, turned upside down and sideways. I was in such agony because I was sure I was going back inside!

I stood before Judge Hamilton (I know he won't believe I still remember his name. The man made an *impression* on me!), the same judge who sent Darryl up. I knew who he was and, worse, he knew who I was. He was angry because my school record was so good, and he let me know it. He looked me straight in the eye and said, "You're not doing anything but conning your mother and now you're trying to con me, because we both know you know how to do the right thing."

I was scared as hell, man. The judge continued to give me a good old-fashioned tongue-lashing in his court, which to this day I can still hear in my head, especially when he looked at me and pulled the big switch. "I'm gonna let you go home, boy."

What?! My stomach did a *whoommp*! I couldn't believe what I was hearing.

He went on. "Just remember, son, I'm gonna be your judge from now on, whenever you get in trouble. If you come back before me for so much as a jaywalking ticket you'll have twenty-two months to think about it." He stared at me coldly, pounded his gavel, and said loud and with authority, "Probation for a year! Next case!"

I walked out of that courtroom with a big smile on my face. I passed through the same gate I'd heard slamming on me when I was going in, only this time it was slamming behind me. That same noise, *whhhhrraaaaaahhhh!*, but I liked it so much better from the outside. I knew I was never going back in, that the life I'd known on the street, all of it was history. I was going to change everything because the night before I'd heard the *Voice and the Voice had heard me!*

BARRY WHITE,
from *Love Unlimited*

CHILDREN OF THE SUN

❧

WE ARE CHILDREN of the sun and our race has a definite tradition of beauty and glory and vitality that is as rich and powerful as the sun itself. These traditions are ours to express and will enrich our careers in proportion to the sincerity and faithfulness with which we interpret them.

DUKE ELLINGTON

THE FLOOD

A PREACHER was walking down the road one day when a nearby dam burst. As the water reached the preacher's ankles, a car drove up.

"Preacher, get in before the water rises," the driver said.

"That's all right," the preacher said. "God will look out for me."

The driver drove on.

The preacher continued to walk, and the water continued to rise until it reached his hips. A woman in a rowboat paddled by.

"Preacher, jump in my boat before the water rises," said the woman.

"That's all right," the preacher said. "God will look out for me."

The woman rowed on.

The preacher continued until the water reached his

neck. A helicopter flew by and the copilot threw down a rope.

"Preacher, climb up before the water rises," said the copilot.

"That's all right," the preacher said. "God will look out for me."

The helicopter flew away.

Finally the water rose over the preacher's head and he drowned. In heaven, he stood before the Lord.

"Dear God," the preacher said. "I was a good man. I was true to Your commandments and good, kind, and loving to my fellow man. Why didn't You save me?"

The Lord looked at him and said, "Well, first I sent you a car, then I sent you a boat, then I sent you a helicopter . . ."

S H A R O N   D A V I S

REVELATION

※

I

T STARTED OUT as an average day at Seventy-
fourth Street elementary school in Los Angeles, but
it turned out to be a day that changed my life. I was
no more than seven or eight years old—more likely six
or seven—and we were talking about what we wanted to
be when we grow up. The teacher, whose curly mass of
graying red hair and brogue testified that she was from
Ireland, listened with a smile on her face as the kids in
my class, which I remember as being a mix of black and
white, spoke about their dreams. When it came my turn,
I said I wanted to be a writer. When she heard this, her
face fell, and she looked at me, puzzled. She recovered
her smile and allowed me to finish. On my way out the
door to lunch, she pulled me aside. She said she didn't
think that was such a good idea—me wanting to be a
writer. She said that black people—we were called

Negroes at that time, the early sixties—just couldn't be writers. "It's nothing personal," she said in her melodious brogue. "It's just that every group has its talent, and for your people that talent is singing and dancing, not writing." So, she concluded, I should put aside all thought of writing for a living.

That night I happened to mention the incident to my grandmother, who was cooking dinner while my mother was out on an acting job and my father was at his real estate office. I told my grandmother not as a complaint, but simply as one of the things that happened today at school. I was only trying to make conversation. But when I told her about the teacher's comment, my grandmother stopped chopping the celery and carrots and turned toward me. She squatted so that she would be face-to-face with me, and a fire burned in her eyes. She grabbed my shoulders with both hands, squeezing so hard that it hurt.

"Ricky," she said, calling me by my nickname. "Never let anybody tell you who you are, what you like, or what you can be. You alone be the judge of that. You alone determine that. Forget about what that teacher said. If you want to be a writer, get yourself a paper and pencil and get to work." She then released me, stood up, and returned to her cooking. We never spoke about the incident again.

Since that time I have heard or read similar comments by teachers and counselors, in *The Autobiography of Malcolm X* and in an interview given by the author James Baldwin on PBS. So the teacher's reaction was nothing new and I was not alone. But to this day, nearly forty years later, it is my grandmother's words that cling to me with an awesome force. And to this day, I can still feel on my shoulders the viselike strength of her grip.

ERIC V. COPAGE

RECIPE FOR FAITH

THE SAYING is that God helps those who help themselves. And more times than not this is correct. Of course, things do happen in mysterious ways. There are miracles. Ask Joan of Arc, a fifteenth-century peasant girl who got the ear of the king of France. Ask me. Twenty years ago, when I was short on my rent and down on my luck, I was wandering along the street worrying about what I would do. Suddenly, out of the corner of my eye, I saw a cylindrical shape about the size of a tube for toilet paper. It was a thick wad of bills. I picked it up and counted it: four hundred dollars and change, which just about covered that month's rent. Go ahead, shake your head and suck your teeth. It happened. Even I had a hard time believing it. But even with miracles, it is important to be prepared. What good is it if a miracle should present a much-needed horse, but you cannot ride. What good is it if a miracle should present a much-needed book, but you cannot read. What good is it to hit the lottery, if you don't know how to wisely invest the money. So, the foundation of faith is preparedness. But even then, faith is a composite of so many other things. Such as . . .

Love: The faith that God's goodness will seek you out no matter where you are.

Self-Esteem: The faith that you can do whatever you set your mind to.

Family: The faith that there are supportive people who believe in you and will support you as you try to realize your dreams.

Creativity: The faith that you can turn any situation to your advantage.

Tenacity: The faith that you can be either the Rock of Gibraltar when necessary or an autumn leaf if the situation demands it.

Wisdom: The faith that you will know when to be a rock and when to be a leaf.

Faith: The faith that even without any of the above, miracles do happen.

ERIC V. COPAGE

AFTERWORD

I HOPE that you've liked this book, whether you've read it cover to cover like a seven-course meal, or whether you chose to pick at it like a buffet. But I'd like to leave you with some final thoughts—desserts, if you will—and it is my hope that these will help inspire us to show solidarity and to affirm ourselves and our heritage. Time is growing short, and we can't wait for the perfect moment. Now is the time to act. Now is the time to take the first steps:

Now is the time to look at the first black person you see and say, "Hello black woman, your wisdom is deeper than the deepest ocean, and I do believe that you can do anything you put your mind to."

Now is the time to look at the first black person you see and say, "Hello black man, you are more brilliant that a thousand suns, and I do believe that you can do anything you put your mind to."

Now is the time to look at the first black child you see and say, "You are my child. And if you stumble, I'll support you. And if you fall, I'll pick you up. Because you are my child, and I believe in you. You are the future of our race, and I believe in the future of our race."

Now is the time. Not next year in hopes of finding a new black organization. Not six months from now in hopes of finding a new black leader. Not tomorrow after we've filled our bellies and quenched our thirst. But now. Today. Right now . . .

Now is the time to look into the mirror and to pledge to do at least one thing today toward realizing one goal. Now is the time to look at our kente cloth, family photographs, and other symbols of black pride and let those inspire us to excellence.

Now is the time to get to work. Now is the time to put our shoulder to the wheel. Now is the time to remember a time when someone told us we couldn't do something—and we proved them wrong.

Now is the time to thank our wives and husbands, mothers and fathers, brothers and sisters, aunts and uncles—and strangers, too—for showing us their support.

Now is the time to look at our black skin, our woolly hair, our wide noses, and full lips and to say "these are the marks of genius."

Now is the time to exercise and eat right so that we might become strong members of our race.

Now is the time to celebrate the good in us. Now is the time to focus on our aspirations. Because now is the time to stand up. Now is the time to stand up and be the black men and women the Good Lord meant us to be.

ACKNOWLEDGMENTS

I AM IN DEBT to friends and family who have given me a lifetime of love, emotional support, and spiritual guidance through their narratives. Over the years these stories have buoyed me through bad times and enhanced my appreciation of life during good times. But it is impossible to give credit to the many miniconversations and late-night talks—the many chronicles, long and short, humorous and poignant—that inspired this book, so I will restrict myself to thanking by name the following: Thank you, Ellen Archer and Navorn Johnson for your generosity, good wishes, and belief in the project, and help in getting it done; thank you, Beverly Rena Bell, David Cashion, Doris Cooper, and Debra Murphy for your excellent research; thank you, John R. Long for your help with the Aesop fables; thank you, Mark Chait for your conscientious administrative work and for your perseverance in securing permission to use much of the material in this book; thank you, Gwen Smith for typing out these stories. And grand thanks to you, Will Schwalbe, for your vision, resourcefulness, faith, and adroit pencil work.

TELL US YOUR STORY

THE SELECTIONS in this book were, of course, highly personal, comprised of tales and poems that have touched me and my circle of friends and acquaintances. These stories are not meant to be the last word on our lore. I am eager to receive your contributions for future editions of *Soul Food*. You can submit as many stories as you want and on any subject. The contribution can be comical or heartbreaking, wry or eerie. It can be a family story or a story a friend told you. It can be something that happened years ago or only a few minutes ago. But the story must be of your own invention or from your own life. As for length, anything up to two hand- or type-written pages will do. You can e-mail the story to copage@home.com or mail it to me care of Hyperion (see page iv for the address).

We all have so much to learn from each other, and so much comfort and inspiration to offer each other. Thanks in advance for adding your voice.

CREDITS

"Hungry for Airtime" from *Live Your Dreams* by Les Brown. Copyright © 1992 by Les Brown Unlimited, Inc. Reprinted by permission of HarperCollins Publishers, Inc.

"Jennifer Holliday" by Jacqueline Jones LaMon. Copyright © 1999. Reprinted by permission of the author.

"The Shiny Red Bicycle" by Jon Haggins. Copyright © 1999. Reprinted by permission of the author.

"Self-Doubt" from *Love Unlimited: Insights on Life and Love* by Barry White, copyright © 1999 by Barry White. Used by permission of Broadway Books, a division of Random House, Inc.

"Coming to Terms with the J-j-jitters" by Michael E. Ross. Copyright © 1989. Reprinted by permission of the author.

"Lessons of the River" from *Southern Journey: A Return to the Civil Rights Movement* by Tom Dent. Copyright © 1997 by Tom Dent. Reprinted by permission of HarperCollins Publishers, Inc.

"A Giant Step" by Henry Louis Gates Jr. Copyright © 1990 by Henry Louis Gates Jr. Originally published in *The New York Times Magazine*. Reprinted by permission of the author.

"Marathon Woman" reprinted from *Make the Connection: Ten Steps to a Better Body—and a Better Life* by Bob Greene and Oprah Winfrey. Copyright © 1996 Harpo, Inc. and Bob Greene and Oprah Winfrey. Published by Hyperion.

"A Christmas Carol" from *Mississippi: An American Journey* by Anthony Walton. Copyright © 1996 by Anthony Walton. Reprinted by permission of Alfred A. Knopf, a Division of Random House Inc.